FOG AND CLOUD COMPUTING

Sankari M. | Kamatchi K.S. | P. Jeyanthi

KHANNA BOOK PUBLISHING CO. (P) Ltd.
4C/4344, Ansari Road, Darya Ganj, New Delhi, India

Sathyabama Institute of Science and Technology
Jeppiaar Nagar, Rajiv Gandhi Salai, Chennai, Tamilnadu, India

Dear Readers,

To prevent the piracy, this book is secured with HIGH SECURITY HOLOGRAM on the front title cover. In case you don't find the hologram on the front cover title, please write us to at contact@khannabooks.com or whatsapp us at +91-99109 09320 and avail special gift voucher for yourself.

Specimen of Hologram on front Cover title:

Moreover, there is a SPECIAL DISCOUNT COUPON for you with EVERY HOLOGRAM.

How to avail this SPECIAL DISCOUNT:

Step 1: Scratch the hologram
Step 2: Under the scratch area, your "coupon code" is available
Step 3: Logon to www.khannabooks.com
Step 4: Use your "coupon code" in the shopping cart and get your copy at a special discount
Step 5: Enjoy your reading!

Thanks,
Khanna Publishing House

ISBN: 978-93-55382-39-9

FOG AND CLOUD COMPUTING
by **Sankari M. | Kamatchi K.S. | P. Jeyanthi**

First Edition: 2025
Reprint: 2026

To view complete list of books, please scan the QR Code:

Published by:
Khanna Book Publishing Co. (P) Ltd.
CIN: U22110DL1998PTC095547

Visit us at: www.khannabooks.com
Write us at: contact@khannabooks.com

Printed in Bharat.

Preface

By the world rapidly changes of the information technology, Cloud computing has revolutionized the drastic change in the technology field. With the rapid growth of the digital age, cloud computing is the foundation of modern infrastructure, providing industry flexibility, efficiency and innovation. By the way businesses, individuals and organizations approach technology , provide scalable on-demand computer resources on the Internet.

As a server, memory, databases, applications, and network services over the Internet, Cloud computing allows users to store and process data on remote servers hosted by various service providers, instead of relying on physical hardware and data centers.

Next, book chapter focuses a variety of services, virtualization and security available in the cloud, such as AWS, Google, and Microsoft, and deployment models.

This book focuses on the adoption of cloud computing as a key driver of digital transformation in businesses, providing new opportunities for remote work, global collaboration and data-managed decision-making. Using cloud infrastructure allows businesses to stay agile, innovate faster, and respond quickly to changing market conditions. Rather than relying solely on remote cloud data centers for data processing, storage, and analysis, we provide a more detailed explanation of where data is generated.

If fog and cloud computing is developed, it will transform the technical situation and whether it is in the world of personal growth, professional growth, or simply open collaboration, the importance of the future of computers and cloud computing. The book aims to give them the basic foundation of cloud computing for being part of this exciting and dynamic area.

As Fog and cloud computing continues to evolve, it is reshaping the technological landscape and establishing itself as an essential part of the future of computing.

We hope that this book will serve as a valuable resource for anyone interested in fog and cloud computing, whether for personal development, professional growth, or simply to explore the world of open collaboration. The open-source movement is constantly evolving, and this book aims to give you the foundation to be a part of this exciting and dynamic field.

Happy Reading and Contributing to Cloud computing!

Preface

Contents

UNIT 1

Understanding Cloud Computing

1.1 History of Cloud Computing

Before emerging the cloud computing, there was Client/Server computing which is basically a centralized storage in which all the software applications, all the data and all the controls are resided on the server side. If a single user wants to access specific data or run a program, he/she need to connect to the server and then gain appropriate access, and then he/she can do his/her business. Then after, distributed computing came into picture, where all the computers are networked together and share their resources when needed. On the basis of above computing, there was emerged of cloud computing concepts that later implemented.

At around in 1961, John Mac Charty suggested in a speech at MIT that computing can be sold like a utility, just like a water or electricity. It was a brilliant idea, but like all brilliant ideas, it was ahead if its time, as for the next few decades, despite interest in the model, the technology simply was not ready for it. But of course time has passed and the technology caught that idea and after few years we mentioned that:

In 1999, Salesforce.com started delivering of applications to users using a simple website. The applications were delivered to enterprises over the Internet, and this way the dream of computing sold as utility were true.

In 2002, Amazon started Amazon Web Services, providing services like storage, computation and even human intelligence. However, only starting with the launch of the Elastic Compute Cloud in 2006 a truly commercial service open to everybody existed.

In 2009, Google Apps also started to provide cloud computing enterprise applications. same year Microsoft launched Windows Azure, and companies like Oracle and HP have all joined the game. This proves that today, cloud computing has become mainstream.

1.2 Characteristics of Cloud Computing

The characteristics of cloud computing are given below:

1. Agility

The cloud works in the distributed computing environment. It shares resources among users and works very fast.

2. High Availability and Reliability

Availability of servers is high and more reliable, because chances of infrastructure failure are minimal.

3. High Scalability

Means "on-demand" provisioning of resources on a large scale, without having engineers for peak loads.

4. Multi-Sharing

With the help of cloud computing, multiple users and applications can work more efficiently with cost reductions by sharing common infrastructure.

5. Device and Location Independence

Cloud computing enables the users to access systems using a web browser regardless of their location or what device they use e.g. PC, mobile phone etc. As infrastructure is off-site (typically provided by a third-party) and accessed via the Internet, users can connect from anywhere.

6. Maintenance

Maintenance of cloud computing applications is easier, since they do not need to be installed on each user's computer and can be accessed from different places. So, it reduces the cost also.

7. Low Cost

By using cloud computing, the cost will be reduced because to take the services of cloud computing, IT company need not to set its own infrastructure and pay as per usage of resources.

8. Services in pay-per-use mode

Application Programming Interfaces (APIs) are provided to the users so that they can access services on the cloud by using these APIs and pay the charges as per the usage of services.

1.3 Architectural Framework

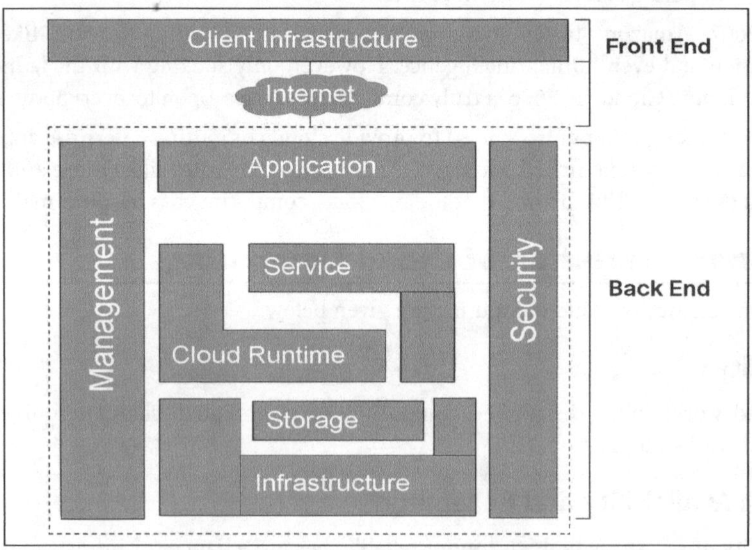

Fig. 1.1: Cloud Computing Architecture

Cloud Computing architecture (Figure 1.1) refers to the various components and sub- components of cloud that constitute the structure of the system.

Cloud computing architecture consists of:

a. A front-end platform that can include fat clients, thin clients, and mobile devices
b. Back-end platforms, such as servers and storage
c. Cloud-based delivery
d. A network (internet, intranet)

At its most basic, cloud architecture can be classified into two sections: front-end and back- end, connected to each other via a virtual network or the internet. There are other parts of cloud architecture including middleware, cloud resources, etc., but for now we'll just review the basics.

1.3.1 Front End Cloud Computing

Front-end is the side that is visible to the client, customer, or user. Front-end pieces include the user interface, and the client's computer system or network that is used for accessing the cloud system. You have probably noticed that different cloud computing systems use different user interfaces—for example, not only can you choose from a variety of web browsers (including Chrome, Safari, Firefox, etc.), but the Google Docs user interface is different than that of Salesforce.

1.3.2 Back End Cloud Computing

On the other hand, the back-end pieces are on the side used by the service provider. These include various servers, computers, data storage systems, virtual machines, and programs that together constitute the cloud of computing services. The back-end side also is responsible for providing security mechanisms, traffic control and protocols that connect networked computers for communication.

To briefly summarize: the front-end is the part you see, and the back-end is the computing that happens behind the scenes.

1.3.3 Cloud Based Delivery

As we've discussed above, cloud computing services are everywhere these days. For example, if your company uses Salesforce or QuickBooks—or you use Google Drive or Office 365 at home or work, you're a cloud computing user. These are all examples of subscriptions a company or individual can purchase that enable them to use the software, typically known as Software-as-a-Service, or SaaS.

Because of technology like virtualization and hypervisors, it's possible for many virtual servers to exist on a single physical server. These technologies power other cloud subscriptions like Platform-as-a-Service (PaaS), Infrastructure-as-a-Service (IaaS), and more.

1.3.4 Cloud Services Network

Cloud services can be delivered publicly or privately using the internet and can also remain within a company's network when delivered over an intranet. Sometimes, organizations make use of a combination of both.

No matter where the actual "cloud" is—a company's own data center or a service provider's data center, cloud computing uses networking to enable convenient, on -

demand access toa shared pool of computing resources like networks, storage, servers, services, and applications. By using virtualization, these assets can be provisioned and released quickly and easily as necessary.

1.4 Types of cloud

1.4.1 Public Cloud

Public cloud allows the accessibility of systems and services easily to general public. E.g.: Amazon, IBM, Microsoft, Google, Rackspace etc.

1.4.2 Advantages of Public Cloud Model

1. Low Cost

Public cloud is having low cost as compared to private or hybrid cloud, because it shares same resources with large number of consumers.

2. Reliable

Public cloud provides large number of resources from different locations, if any of the resource fail, public cloud can employ another one.

3. Flexible

It is very easy to integrate public cloud with private cloud and hence it gives flexible approach to consumers.

4. Location Independent

It ensures the independency of location, because public cloud services are delivered through Internet.

5. High Scalability

Cloud resources are available as per the demand from the pool of resources that means they can be scaled up or down according to the requirements.

1.4.3 Disadvantages of Public Cloud Model

1. Low Security

In public cloud model, data is present off-site and resources are shared publicly. Hence it does not ensure the high level security.

2. Less Customizable

It is less customizable than private cloud.

1.5 Private Cloud

The Private cloud allows the accessibility of systems and services within the organization. Private cloud is operated only within a particular organization. But it will be managedinternally or by third party.

1.5.1 Advantages of Private Cloud Model

1. High security and privacy

Private cloud resources are shared from distinct pool of resources and hence highly secured.

2. More Control

Private clouds have more control on its resources and hardware than public cloud because it is accessed only within the boundary of an organization.

1.5.2 Disadvantages of Private Cloud Model

1. Restriction

Private cloud is only accessible locally and it is very difficult to deploy globally.

2. More Cost

Cloud is having more cost than public clouds.

3. Inflexible Price

In order to fulfill demands, purchasing new hardware is very costly.

4. Less Scalability

Private clouds are scaled only within capacity of internal hosted resources.

1.6 Hybrid Cloud

The Hybrid cloud is the mixture of public and private cloud. Non-critical activities are performed by public cloud while critical activities are performed by private cloud.

1.6.1 Advantages of Hybrid Cloud Model

1. Scalable

It provides both the features of public and private cloud scalability.

2. Flexible and secure

It provides secure resources because of private cloud and scalable resources because of public cloud.

3. Cost effective

It is having less cost as compared to private cloud.

1.6.2 Disadvantages of Hybrid Cloud Model

1. Networking issues

Networking becomes complex because of private and public cloud.

2. Security Compliance

It is necessary to ensure that cloud services are compliant with the security policies of an organization.

1.7 Pros and Cons of Cloud

1.7.1 Advantages of Cloud Computing

There are various advantages of cloud computing technology. The important advantages of cloud computing are given below.

1. Lower cost computer for users

In cloud, you don't require a high-powered (and accordingly high-priced) computer to run cloud computing's web based applications because applications run on cloud not ondesktop PC or laptop.

2. Lower IT infrastructure cost

By using cloud computing, you need not to invest in larger numbers of more powerful servers, you also need not to require the IT staff for handling such powerful servers.

3. Fewer maintenance cost

The maintenance cost in cloud computing greatly reduces both hardware and software maintenance for organizations of all sizes.

4. Lower Software Cost

It reduces the software cost because you don't need to purchase separate softwarepackages for each computer in the organization.

5. Instant software updates

Another software-related advantage in cloud computing is that users don't need to face with the choice between obsolete software and high upgrade costs. If the app is web- based, updates happen automatically and are available next time when the user logs in to the cloud.

6. Increased computing Power

The execution capacity of cloud servers are very high. It processes the application veryfast.

7. Unlimited storage capacity

Cloud offers you a huge amount of storage capacity like 2000 GB or more than that if required.

1.7.2 Disadvantages of Cloud Computing

There are various disadvantages of cloud computing technology. The important disadvantages of cloud computing are given below.

1. Require a constant Internet Connection

Cloud computing is impossible without Internet connection. To access any applications and documents you need a constant Internet connection.

2. Require High Speed Internet connection

Similarly, a low-speed Internet connection makes cloud computing painful at best and often impossible. Web based apps often require a lot of bandwidth to download, as need todownload large documents.

3. Stored Data Might Not Be Secure

With cloud computing, all your data is stored in the cloud. That's all well and good, but how secure is the cloud? Can't unauthorized users gain access to your confidential data.

1.8 Differences between Cloud and Web 2.0

Table 1.1: Differences between Cloud vs Web 2.0

S.No.	Cloud Computing	Web 2.0
1.	It is more specific and definite	Programming and business models
2.	It is a way of searching through data.	It is sharing entire pieces of data between different websites.
3.	Cloud computing is about computers.	Web 2.0 is about people.
4.	The internet as a computing platform	Attempt to explore and explain the business rules of that platform
5.	Google apps are considered in Cloud computing.	A web-based application is considered in Web 2.0.
6.	It is a business model for hosting these services.	It is a technology which allows webpages to act as more responsive applications

1.9 Challenges in Cloud Computing

Cloud computing is used for enabling global access to mutual pools of resources such as services, apps, data, servers, and computer networks. It is done on either a third-party server located in a data center or a privately owned cloud. This makes data-accessing contrivances more reliable and efficient, with nominal administration effort.

Because cloud technology depends on the allocation of resources to attain consistency and economy of scale, similar to a utility, it is also fairly cost-effective, making it the choice for many small businesses and firms. But there are also many challenges involved in cloud computing, and if you're not prepared to deal with them, you won't realize the benefits. Here are six common challenges you must consider before implementing cloud computing technology.

1. Cost

Cloud computing itself is affordable, but tuning the platform according to the company's needs can be expensive. Furthermore, the expense of transferring the data to public cloudscan prove to be a problem for short-lived and small-scale projects. Companies can save some money on system maintenance, management, and acquisitions.But they also have to invest in additional bandwidth, and the absence of routine control in an infinitely scalable computing platform can increase costs.

2. Service Provider Reliability

The capacity and capability of a technical service provider are as important as price. The service provider must be available when you need them. The main concern should be the service provider's sustainability and reputation. Make sure you comprehend the techniques via which a provider observes its services and defends dependability claims.

3. Downtime

Downtime is a significant shortcoming of cloud technology. No seller can promise a platform that is free of possible downtime. Cloud technology makes small companies reliant on their connectivity, so companies with an untrustworthy internet connection probably want to think twice before adopting cloud computing.

4. Password Security

Industrious password supervision plays a vital role in cloud security. However, the more people you have accessing your cloud account, the less secure it is. Anybody aware of your passwords will be able to access the information you store there.

Businesses should employ multi-factor authentication and make sure that passwords are protected and altered regularly, particularly when staff members leave. Access rights related to passwords and usernames should only be allocated to those who require them.

5. Data privacy

Sensitive and personal information that is kept in the cloud should be defined as being for internal use only, not to be shared with third parties. Businesses must have a plan to securely and efficiently manage the data they gather.

6. Vendor lock-in

Entering a cloud computing agreement is easier than leaving it. "Vendor lock-in" happens when altering providers is either excessively expensive or just not possible. It could be that the service is nonstandard or that there is no viable vendor substitute. It comes down to buyer carefulness. Guarantee the services you involve are typical and transportable to other providers, and above all, understand the requirements. Cloud computing is a good solution for many businesses, but it's important to know what you're getting into. Having plans to address these six prominent challenges first will help ensure a successful experience.

1.10 Cloud Players

There are top 5 cloud players

1. Microsoft

Microsoft remains an absolute lock at the top due to four factors: its deep involvement at all three layers of the cloud (IaaS, PaaS and SaaS); its unmatched commitment to developing and helping customers deploy AI, ML and Blockchain in innovative production environments; its market-leading cloud revenue, which I estimate at about $16.7 billion for the trailing 12 months (***not*** to be confused with the forward-projected $20.4 billion annualized run rate the company released on Oct. 26); and the extraordinary vision and leadership of CEO Satya Nadella.

2. Amazon

Amazon might not have the end-to-end software chops of the others in the Top 5 but it was and continues to be the poster-child for the cloud-computing movement: the first-movingparadigm- buster and category creator. I believe Amazon will make some big moves to bolsterits position in software, and no matter how you slice it, the $16 billion in trailing-12-month cloud revenue from AWS is awfully impressive.

3. IBM

IBM has leapfrogged both Salesforce.com (formerly tied with Amazon for #2 and now in the #4 spot) and SAP (formerly #4) on the strength of its untrendy but highly successful emphasis on transforming its vast array of software expertise and technology from the on- premises world to the cloud. In so doing, IBM has quietly created a $15.8-billion cloud business (again on trailing-12-month basis) that includes revenue of $7 billion from helping big global corporations convert legacy systems to cloud or cloud-enabled environments. And like #1 Microsoft, IBM plays in all three layers of the cloud—IaaS, PaaS and SaaS—which is hugely important for the elite cloud vendors because it allows them to give customers more choices, more seamless integration, better cyber security, and more reasons for third-party developers to rally to the IBM Cloud. Plus, its relentless pairing of "cloud and cognitive" is an excellent approach toward weaving AI and ML deeply into customer-facing solutions.

4. Salesforce.com

Salesforce.com falls a couple of spots from its long-time tie with Amazon at #2 but—and this will be the case as long as founder Marc Benioff is CEO—remains a powerful source of digital innovation and disruptive strategy. However, to remain in the rarified air near the top of the Cloud Wars Top 10, Benioff and Salesforce must find a way to extend their market impactbeyond their enormously successful SaaS business and become more of a high-impact player in the platform or PaaS space. At this stage, it's simply not possible for Salesforce to become a player in IaaS, so Benioff needs to crank up the genius machine and hammer his way into top contention as a platform powerhouse.

5. SAP

SAP has what all of the other cloud vendors would kill for: unmatched incumbency within all of the world's leading corporations as the supplier of mission-critical business applications that run those companies. It's also fashioned, under CEO Bill Mc Dermott, powerful new partnerships with Amazon and Google to complement its long-standing relationships with IBM and Microsoft, all of which give customers a heightened sense of confidence that SAP will be willing and able to play nice in heterogeneous environments. Plus, SAP's HANA technology is now in full deployment across thousands of businesses, and as it takes root and SAP continues to rationalize its massive product portfolio around HANA in the cloud, SAP has a very bright future ahead of it in the cloud.

1.11 Deployment Models

As the cloud technology is providing users with so many benefits, these benefits must have to be categorized based on users requirement. Cloud deployment model represents the exact category of cloud environment based on proprietorship, size, and access and also describes the nature and purpose of the cloud. Most organizations implement the cloud infrastructure to minimize capital expenditure & regulate operating costs.

The National Institute of Standards and Technology (NIST) is an agency under the scope of US Department of Commerce which is responsible for expounding & defining standards in Science and Technology. The Computer Security Division of NISD has provided a formal definition of Cloud computing. The US government is a major consumer of computer technology and also one of the major cloud computing network users.

According to the NIST working definition of cloud, deployment model is one of the two categories of model illustrated by NIST. The NIST model doesn't require a cloud technology to use virtualization to share resources. Cloud support multi-tenancy; multi-tenancy is the concept of sharing of resources among two or more clients. The latest NIST model of cloud computing requires virtualization and utilizes the concept of multi-tenancy.

As the cloud computing us approaching towards a set of interacting components, such as Service-oriented Architecture, users can expect the future versions of the NIST model may include more features also.

1.11.1 Various Deployment Model

To know which deployment model matches your requirement and desire, it is necessary for users as well as learners to understand the four sub-categories of models for deployment.

1.11.1.1 Public Cloud

Public Cloud is a type of cloud hosting that allows the accessibility of systems & its services to its clients/users easily. Some of the examples of those companies which provide public cloud facilities are IBM, Google, Amazon, Microsoft, etc. This cloud service is open for use. This type of cloud computing is a true specimen of cloud hosting where the service providers render services to various clients. From the technical point of view, there is the least difference between private clouds and the public clouds along with the structural design. Only the security level

The advantages of the Public cloud are:

- Flexible
- Reliable
- High Scalable
- Low cost
- Place independence

This type also holds some disadvantages such as:

- Less Secured
- Poor Customizable

1.11.1.2 Private Cloud

Private Cloud also termed as 'Internal Cloud'; which allows the accessibility of systems and services within a specific boundary or organization. The cloud platform is implemented in a cloud-based secure environment that is guarded by advanced firewalls under the surveillance of the IT department that belongs to a particular organization. Private clouds permit only authorized users, providing the organizations greater control over data and its security.Business organizations that have dynamic, critical, secured, management demand basedrequirement should adopt Private Cloud.

The advantages of using private cloud are:

- **Highly private and secured:** Private cloud resource sharing is highly secured.
- **Control Oriented:** Private clouds provide more control over its resources than public cloud as it can be accessed within the organization's boundary.

The disadvantages of using Private cloud:

- **Poor scalability:** Private type of clouds is scaled within internal limited hosted resources.
- **Costly:** As it provides secured and more features, so it's more expensive than a public cloud.
- **Pricing:**is inflexible; i.e., purchasingnew hardwarefor up-gradation is morecostly.
- **Restriction:** It can be accessed locally within an organization and is difficult to expose globally.

1.11.1.3 Hybrid Cloud

Hybrid Cloud is another cloud computing type, which is integrated, i.e., it can be a combination of two or more cloud servers, i.e., private, public or community combined as one architecture, but remain individual entities.

Non-critical tasks such as development and test workloads can be done using public cloud whereas critical tasks that are sensitive such as organization data handling are done using a private cloud. Benefits of both deployment models, as well as community deployment model, are possible in a hybrid cloud hosting. It can cross globally. Sensitive data such as organization data handling are done using a private cloud.

Advantages of Hybrid Cloud Computing are:

- Flexible
- Secure
- Cost Effective
- Rich Scalable

Disadvantages of Hybrid Cloud are:

- Complex networking problem
- Organization's security Compliance

1.11.1.4 Community Cloud

It is another type of cloud computing in which the setup of the cloud is shared manually among different organizations that belong to the same community or area. Example of such a community is where organizations/firms are there along with the financial institutions/ banks. A multi-tenant setup developed using cloud among different organizations that belong to a particular community or group having similar computing concern.

For joint business organizations, ventures, research organizations and tenders community cloud is the appropriate solution. Selection of right type of cloud hosting is essential in this case. Thus, community-based cloud users need to know and analyze the business demand first.

1.12 Virtualization

The term 'Virtualization' can be used in many respect of computer. It is the process of creatinga virtual environment of something which may include hardware platforms, storage devices, OS, network resources, etc.

Virtualization is the ability which allows sharing the physical instance of a single application or resource among multiple organizations or users. This technique is done by assigning a name logically to all those physical resources & provides a pointer to those physical resources based on demand.

Over an existing operating system & hardware, we generally create a virtual machine which and above it we run other operating systems or applications. This is called Hardware Virtualization. The virtual machine provides a separate environment that is logically distinct from its underlying hardware. Here, the system or the machine is the host & virtual machine is the guest machine. This virtual environment is managed by a firmware which is termed as a hypervisor.There are several approaches or ways to virtualizes cloud servers. These are:

a. **Grid Approach:** where the processing workloads are distributed among different physical servers, and their results are then collected as one.

b. **OS - Level Virtualization:** Here, multiple instances of an application can run in an isolated form on a single OS.

c. **Hypervisor-based Virtualization:** which is currently the most widely used technique

With hypervisor's virtualization, there are various sub-approaches to fulfill the goal to run multiple applications & other loads on a single physical host. A technique is used to allow virtual machines to move from one host to another without any requirement of shutting down. This technique is termed as "Live Migration". Another technique is used to actively load balance among multiple hosts to efficiently utilize those resources available in a virtual machine, and the concept is termed as Distributed Resource Scheduling or Dynamic Resource Scheduling.

The virtualization of cloud has been categorized into four different types based on their characteristics. These are:

1. Hardware Virtualization
2. Software Virtualization
3. Server Virtualization
4. OS Virtualization
5. Storage Virtualization

Virtualization plays a significant role in cloud technology and its working mechanism. Usually, what happens in the cloud - the users not only share the data that are located in the cloud like an application but also share their infrastructures with the help of virtualization. Virtualization is used mainly to provide applications with standard versions for the cloud customers & with the release of the latest version of an application the providers can efficiently provide that application to the cloud and its users and it is possible using virtualization only. By the use of this virtualization concept, all servers & software other cloud providers require those are maintained by a third-party, and the cloud provider pays them on a monthly or yearly basis.

In reality, most of the today's hypervisor make use of a combination of different types of hardware virtualization. Mainly virtualization means running multiple systems on a single machine but sharing all resources (hardware) & it helps to share IT resources to get benefit in the business field.

1.12.1 Hardware Virtualization

It is the abstraction of computing resources from the software that uses cloud resources. It involves embedding virtual machine software into the server's hardware components. That software is called the hypervisor. The hypervisor manages the shared physical hardware resources between the guest OS & the host OS. The abstracted hardware is represented as actual hardware. Virtualization means abstraction & hardware virtualization is achieved by abstracting the physical hardware part using Virtual Machine Monitor (VMM) or hypervisor. Hypervisors rely on command set extensions in the processors to accelerate common virtualization activities for boosting the performance. The term hardware virtualization is used when VMM or virtual machine software or any hypervisor gets directly installed on the hardware system. The primary task of the hypervisor is to process monitoring, memory & hardware controlling. After hardware virtualization is done, different operating systems can be installed, and various applications can run on it. Hardware virtualization, when done for server platforms, is also called server virtualization.

Hardware virtualization is of three kinds. These are:

1. **Full Virtualization:** Here the hardware architecture is completely simulated. Guest software doesn't need any modification to run any applications.
2. **Emulation Virtualization:** Here the virtual machine simulates the hardware & is independent. Furthermore, the guest OS doesn't require any modification.
3. **Para-Virtualization:** Here, the hardware is not simulated; instead the guest software runs its isolated system

1.12.2 Software Virtualization

It is also called application virtualization is the practice of running software from a remote server. Software virtualization is similar to that of virtualization except that it is capable to abstract the software installation procedure and create virtual software installation. Many applications & their distributions became typical tasks for IT firms and departments. The mechanism for installing an application differs. So virtualized software is introduced which is an application that will be installed into its self-contained unit and provide software virtualization. Some of the examples are Virtual Box, VMware, etc.The DLL (Data Link Layer) redirect the entire virtualized program's calls to the file system of the server. When the software is run from the server in this procedure, no changes are required to be made on the local system.

- **Ease of Client Deployment:** Virtual software makes it easy to link a file in a network or file copying to the workstation.
- **Software Migration:** Before the concept of virtualization, shifting from one software platform to another was time-consuming; and has a significant impact on the end-systemuser. The software virtualization environment makes migration easier.
- **Easy to Manage:** Application updates become a simple task.

It is the division of physical server into several virtual servers and this division is mainly done to improvise the utility of server resource. In other word it is the masking of resources that are located in server which includes the number & identity of processors, physicalservers & the operating system. This division of one physical server into multiple isolated virtual servers is done by server administrator using software. The virtual environment is sometimes called the virtual private-servers.

1.12.3 Server Virtualization

In this process, the server resources are kept hidden from the user. This partitioning of physical server into several virtual environments; result in the dedication of one server to perform a single application or task.

This technique is mainly used in web-servers which reduces the cost of web-hosting services. Instead of having separate system for each web-server, multiple virtual servers can run on the same system/computer.

The primary uses of server virtualization are:

1. To centralize the server administration
2. Improve the availability of server
3. Helps in disaster recovery
4. Ease in development & testing
5. Make efficient use of server resources.

For Server Virtualization, there are three popular approaches.

These are:

1. Virtual Machine model
2. Para-virtual Machine model

1.12.4 Operating System (OS) Layer Virtualization

Virtualization at OS level functions in a different way and is not based on host-guest paradigm. In this model the host runs a single operating system kernel as its main/core and transfers its functionality to each of the guests. The guest must use the same operating system as the host. This distributed nature of architecture eliminated system calls between layers and hence reduces overhead of CPU usage. It is also a must that each partition remains strictly isolated from its neighbors because any failure or security breach of one partition won't be able to affect the other partitions. There are two levels of OS virtualization.

- **Virtual Machine Model:** are based on host-guest paradigm, where each guest runs on a virtual replica of hardware layer. This technique of virtualization provide guest OS to run without modification. However it requires real computing resources from the host and for this a hypervisor or VM is required to coordinate instructions to CPU.
- **Para-Virtual Machine Model:** is also based on host-guest paradigm & uses virtual machine monitor too. In this model the VMM modifies the guest operating system's code which is called 'porting'. Like that of virtual machine, similarly the Para-virtual machine is alsocapable of executing multiple operating systems. The Para-virtual model is used by both Xen & UML.

1.12.5 Storage Virtualization

It pools the physical storage from different network storage devices and makes it appear to be a single storage unit that is handled from a single console. As we all know there has been a strong bond between physical host & locally installed storage device; and with the change in paradigm, local storage is no longer needed. More advanced storage has come to the market with an increase in functionality. Storage virtualization is the significant component ofstorage servers & facilitates management and monitoring of storage in a virtualized environment.

Storage virtualization helps the storage administrator to backup, archive and recovery data more efficiently, in less amount of time by masking the actual complexity of SAN (Storage Area Network). Through the use of software hybrid appliances, the storage administrator can implement virtualization.

Storage virtualization is becoming more and more important in different forms such as:

- **Storage Tiering:** Using the storage technique as a bridge or as a stepping stone, this technique analyzes and select out the most commonly used data & place it on its highest performing storage pool and the least used data in the weakest performance storage pool.
- **WAN Environment:** Instead of sending multiple copies of the same data over WAN, WAN accelerator is used to locally cache the data and present it in a LAN speed, and not impacting the WAN performance.
- **SAN Storage:** SAN technology present the storage as block-level storage & the storage is presented over the Ethernet network of OS.
- **File Server:** OS writes the data to a remote server location to keep it separate and secure from local users.

Advantages

1. Data is stored in a very convenient location. This is because if the host failure data don't get compromised necessarily.
2. By using storage level abstraction, it becomes flexible how storage is provided, protected, partitioned and used.
3. Storage Devices are capable of performing advanced functions such as disaster recovery, duplication.

As in cloud technology, virtualization plays an important role to make things easy and efficiently done, virtualization also need to be done at the OS level also. With the technique of virtualized OS, nothing is required to be pre-installed or permanently loaded on the local storage device. Everything runs from network using a virtual; simulation & that virtual disk is a disk-image (file) that remotely stored on a server i.e. Storage Area Network (SAN) or Non- Volatile Attached Storage (NAS). It is also called OS-level virtualization is a type of virtualization technology which work on OS layer. Here the kernel of an OS allows more than one isolated user-space instances to exist. Such instances are called containers/ software containers or virtualization engines. In other words, OS kernel will run a single operating system & provide that operating system's functionality to replicate on each of the isolated partitions. It used for virtual hosting environment.It used for securely allocation of finite hardware resources among a large number of distrusting users.System administrator uses it to integrate server hardware by moving services on separate hosts.

To improvised security by separating several applications to several containers.

These forms of virtualization don't require hardware to work efficiently.

The steps for how these virtualization works are listed below:

1. Connect to OS Virtualization Server
2. Connect to virtual disk

3. Then connect this virtual disk to the client
4. OS is streamed to the client
5. If further additional streaming is required, it is done

1.13 Parallelization in Cloud Computing

Parallel computing is a type of computing architecture in which several processorsexecute or process an application or computation simultaneously. Parallel computing helps in performing large computations by dividing the workload between more than one processor, all of which work through the computation at the same time. Most supercomputers implemented parallel computing principles to operate.Parallel computing is also known as parallel processing Parallel processing is generally implemented in operational environments/scenarios that require massive computation or processing power. The primary objective of parallel computing is to increase the available computation power for faster application processing. Typically, parallel computing infrastructure is housed within a single facility where many processors are installed in a server rack or separate servers are connected together.The application server sends a processing request that is distributed in small Component which are concurrently executed on each processor/server. Parallel computation can be classified as bit-level, instructional level, data and task parallelism.

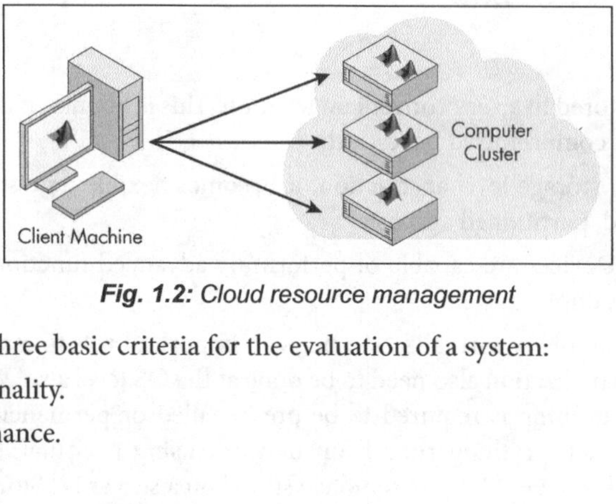

Fig. 1.2: Cloud resource management

It affects the three basic criteria for the evaluation of a system:

1. Functionality.
2. Performance.
3. Cost.

1.14 Cloud resource Management

1.14.1 Cloud Resource

Requires complex policies and decisions for multi-objective optimization.

It is challenging - the complexity of the system makes it impossible tohave accurate global state information affected by unpredictable interactions with the environment,e.g.,system failures, attacks.Cloud service providers are faced with large fluctuating loads whichchallenge the claim of cloud elasticity. The strategies for resource management for IaaS, PaaS, and SaaS are different.

1.14.2 Cloud Resource Management (CRM) Policies

1. **Admission control:** prevent the system from accepting workload inviolation of high-level system policies.

2. **Capacity allocation:** allocate resources for individual activations ofa service.
3. **Load balancing:** distribute the workload evenly among the servers.
4. **Energy optimization:** minimization of energy consumption
5. **Quality of service (QoS) guarantees:** ability to satisfy timing or other conditions specified by a Service Level Agreement

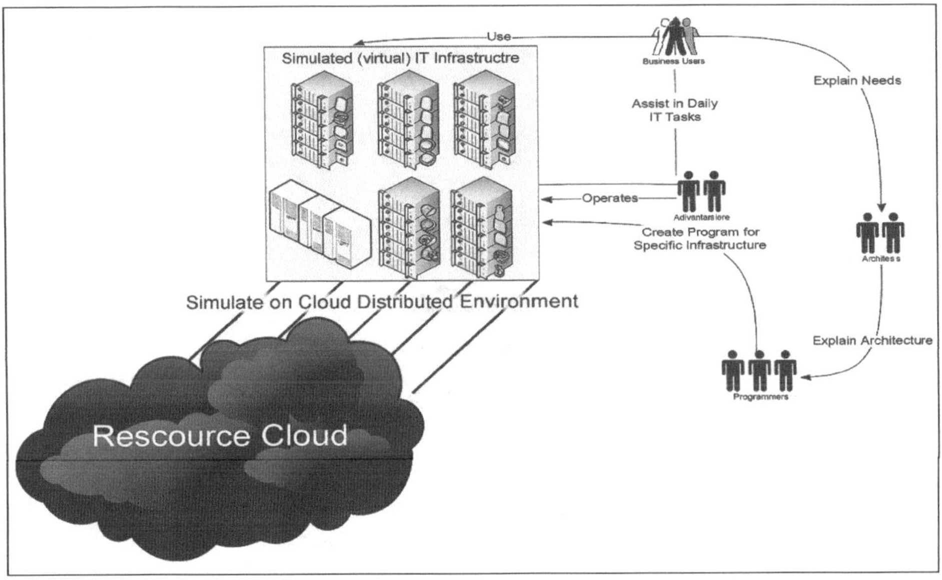

Fig. 1.3: Dynamic resource allocation

Cloud Computing environment can supply of computing resources on the basis of demand and when needed managing the customer demand creates the challenges of on-demand resource allocation.

Effective and dynamic utilization of the resources in cloud can help to balance the load and avoid situations like slow run of systems. Cloud computing allows business outcomes to scale up and down their resources based on needs. Virtual Machines are allocated to the user based on their job in order to reduce the number of physical servers in the cloud environment.

i. If the VM is available then job is allowed to run on the VM.
ii. If the VM is not available then the algorithm finds a low priority job taking into account the job's lease type.
iii. The low priority job is paused its execution by pre-empting its resource.
iv. The high priority job is allowed to run on the resources pre-empted from the low priority.
v. When any other job running on VMs are completed, the job which was paused early can be resumed if the lease type of the job is suspendable.
vi. If not, the suspended job has to wait for the completion of high priority job running in its resources, so that it can be resumed.

There are three types:

- **Cancellable:** These requests can be scheduled at any time after their arrival time.

- **Suspendable:** Suspendable leases are flexible in start time and can be scheduled at any time after their ready time.
- **Non-Preemptable:** The leases associated with such requests cannot be preempted at all.

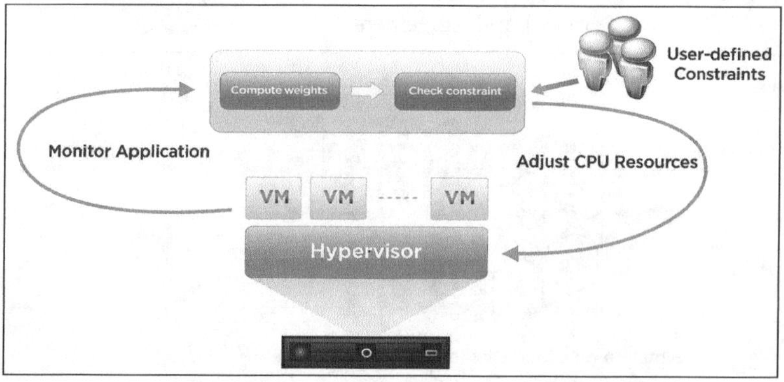

Fig. 1.4: Optimal allocation of cloud models

The optimal allocation of computing resources is a core part for implementing cloud computing.

High heterogeneity, high dynamism, and virtualization make the optimal allocation problem more complex than the traditional scheduling problems in grid system or cloud computing system.

1.15 Cloud Enabling Technology

Cloud-enabling technology refers to the set of tools, platforms, and services that allow organizations to shift their IT infrastructure, data, applications, and services to cloud environments. These technologies support the transition from traditional, on-premise systems to scalable, flexible, and cost-efficient cloud solutions. An overview of key cloud-enabling technologies are

i. Broadband Networks and Internet Architecture
ii. Data Center Technology
iii. Virtualization Technology
iv. Web Technology
v. Multi-tenant Technology
vi. Containerization

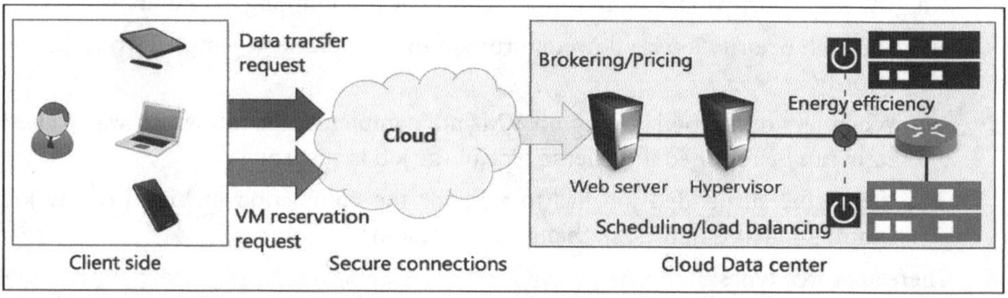

Fig. 1.5: Cloud Enabling Technology

EXERCISE

A. Subjective Questions

1. What is Cloud computing?
2. What are the types of cloud?
3. Describe the architecture of the cloud computing?
4. Differentiate between private cloud,public cloud and community cloud?
5. Discuss the role of companies like Amazon, Google, and Microsoft in shaping modern cloud computing.
6. How do elasticity and resource pooling contribute to efficient cloud services?
7. What are the key components of a cloud computing architecture?
8. What are the challenges faced when implementing a hybrid cloud model?
9. How does cloud computing contribute to cost savings and operational efficiency?
10. 10.What is Web 2.0, and how does it differ from cloud computing?

B. Objective Questions

1. What is cloud computing?
   (a) A type of software
   (b) A type of hardware
   (c) A model for enabling network access to a shared pool of computing resources
   (d) A programming language
2. Which of the following is a key characteristic of cloud computing?
   (a) High latency (b) Resource pooling
   (c) Manual scaling (d) Limited access
3. Which cloud computing model provides only the hardware and allows users to install their operating system and applications?
   (a) Software as a Service (SaaS) (b) Platform as a Service (PaaS)
   (c) Infrastructure as a Service (IaaS) (d) Desktop as a Service (DaaS)
4. Which of the following is NOT a type of cloud deployment model?
   (a) Private cloud (b) Public cloud
   (c) Distributed cloud (d) Hybrid cloud
5. What is the main benefit of using cloud computing?
   (a) Higher electricity costs
   (b) Reduced need for internet connectivity
   (c) On-demand resource availability and scalability
   (d) Increased hardware requirements
6. Which of the following is an example of Software as a Service (SaaS)?
   (a) Microsoft Azure (b) Amazon EC2
   (c) Google Docs (d) Docker

7. What is elasticity in cloud computing?
   (a) The ability to expand and shrink resources as needed
   (b) The use of rubber-based servers
   (c) The method of encrypting data
   (d) The process of hardware replacement
8. Which of the following is a cloud computing security risk?
   (a) High bandwidth
   (b) Data breaches
   (c) Increased uptime
   (d) Scalability
9. What does PaaS provide in cloud computing?
   (a) Physical infrastructure only
   (b) A platform for developing applications without managing the underlying infrastructure
   (c) Ready-to-use software applications
   (d) Network security solutions
10. What does virtualization in cloud computing enable?
   (a) Creation of virtual machines to run multiple operating systems on a single physical machine
   (b) Increasing physical data centers
   (c) Replacing cloud providers
   (d) Eliminating the need for internet access

UNIT 2

Cloud Service Models

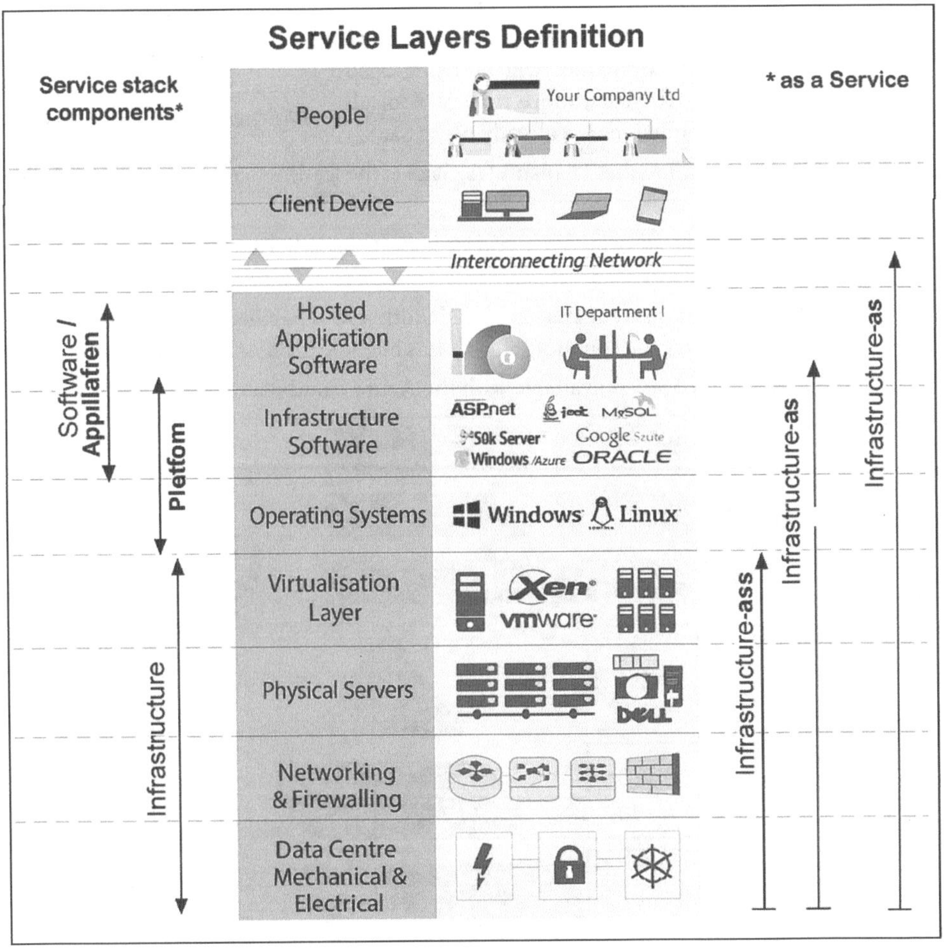

Fig. 2.1: Cloud Services

2.1 Software as a Service

- SaaS (software-as-a-service) is WAN-enabled application services (e.g., Google).
- Software as a Service (SaaS) This is a public cloud service model where the application is 100% managed by the cloud provider.

- SaaS removes the need for organizations to install and run applications on their own computers or in their own data centers.
- This eliminates the expense of hardware acquisition, provisioning and maintenance, as well as software licensing, installation and support.
- Software-as-a-Service (SaaS) has evolved from limited on-line software delivery in 1990s to a fully matured "direct-sourcing" business model for enterprise applications.
- SaaS is one of the fastest growing concepts: more than 10 million companies will be using SaaS in the next 5 - 10 years; more than 50% of all Fortune 500 companies are already using SaaS.

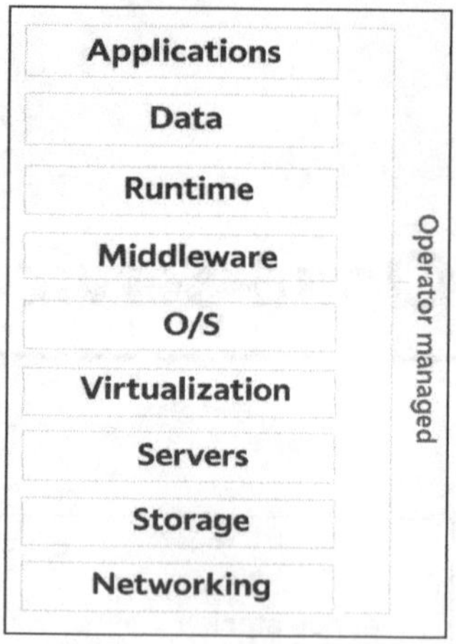

Fig. 2.2: Software as a Service

- According to influential IT institutes, SaaS is the leading business model of choice for 2008/2009
- Virtually all big software/service vendors (IBM, Microsoft, Oracle, Cisco) are investing heavily in SaaS
- With the continuously increasing bandwidth and reliability of the internet, using web services over the (public) internet has become a viable option.
- Microsoft Office 365 is available with the Azure cloud platform.

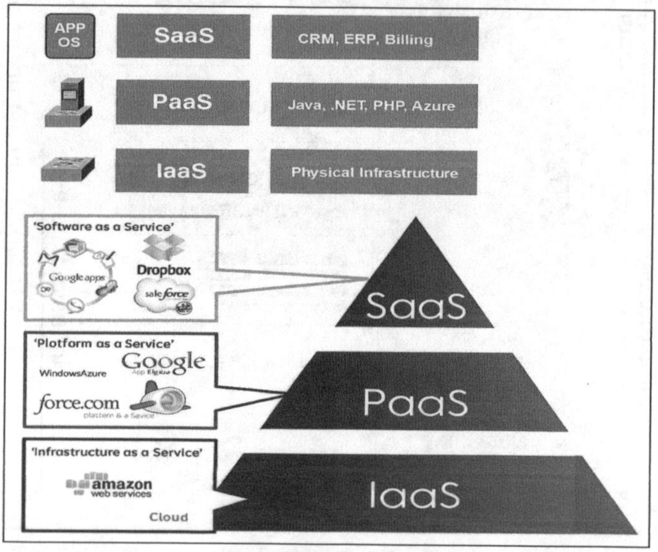

Fig. 2.3: The SPI model

The architecture uses an application instance instead of server instances. There is no actual migration of company servers to the cloud. The SaaS model provides single-tenant and multiple tenant services. The single-tenant dedicates the application instance to the assigned tenant. The multiple tenant application is shared by multiple tenants. The company can manage the security and storage with the single-tenant model. The SaaS application is well suited to internet connectivity. The employees along with their partners and customers can access the application with a variety of network access devices. The SaaS billing model is based on either per usage or monthly subscription. The security compliance requirements for some applications prevented deployment to the SaaS cloud. Some SaaS providers offer Virtual Private SaaS (VPS) services for additional application security. It is a hybrid deployment model that allows peering with an enterprise or VPC database server.

The peering is for storage purposes only and used for security compliance. Salesforce.com is a leading SaaS provider with a CRM application to customers.

Benefits of SaaS

- Flexible payments
- Automatic updates
- On Demand Computing
- Scalable usage
- Accessibility and persistence

Opportunities of SaaS

Software provided as a service by a software vendor to multiple customers with the following main characteristics:

- Standardization of software
- Service including maintenance, support and upgrades
- Web based – usage over the (public) internet
- SaaS offers potential for lowering the Total Cost of Ownership
- Lower operational costs
- No large scale, costly, high risk implementations of applications
- Need few operational resources for application management
- No platform and hardware (maintenance) costs for application servers
- Reduced operational complexity: software delivered as a transparent service through the web
- Minimized software development costs – No lengthy software development and testing cycles
- Lower costs for software use
- No software license and annual maintenance fees
- No expensive software upgrades
- Lower application consultancy and support costs
- SaaS allows corporations to focus on core business activities and responsibilities.
- Transparent overview and usage of electronic data and information
- Automation of iterative, manual tasks
- Faster Time to Market – easy to scale software
- More flexibility in changing and modifying application services for business needs:
- Full scale integration of business processes
  - Control over IT
  - Minimized IT Service Management efforts mainly focused on availability
- Well-defined SLAs between the corporation and the IT vendor
  - More predictable cash flow – easier licensing based on access/usage of software.

- Increased productivity and improved user satisfaction
- Automatic software upgrades withminimal outage

Limitations

Businesses must rely on outside vendors to provide the software, keep that software up and running, track and report accurate billing and facilitate a secure environment for the business data.

2.2 Platform as a Service

1. The Platform as a Service (PaaS) is a way to rent hardware, operating systems, storage and network capacity over the Internet.
2. PaaS services are,
   (a) Data services
   (b) Application runtime
   (c) Messaging & queuing
   (d) Application management.
3. The PaaS is a computing platform that abstracts the infrastructure, OS, and middleware to drive developer productivity.
4. The PaaS is foundational elements to develop new applications

   E.g., Google Application Engine, Microsoft Azure, Coghead.

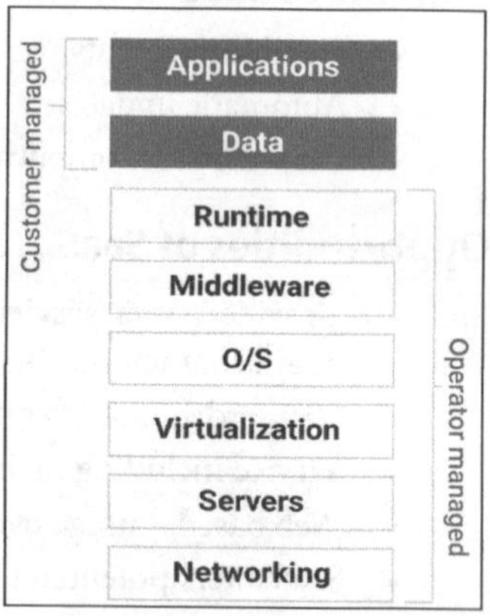

Fig. 2.4: PaaS

5. Add and remove instances based on demand
   (a) Elastic computing!
   (b) Load balancing is part of the Azure fabric and automatically allocate.
6. The PaaS is the delivery of a computing platform and solution stack as a service.

The Solution stack is integrated set of software that provides everything a developer needs to build an application for both software development and runtime.

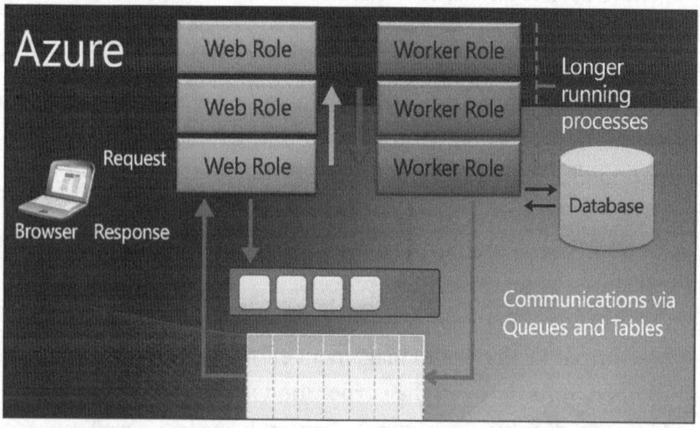

Fig. 2.5: Microsof Azure's Plataform as a Service

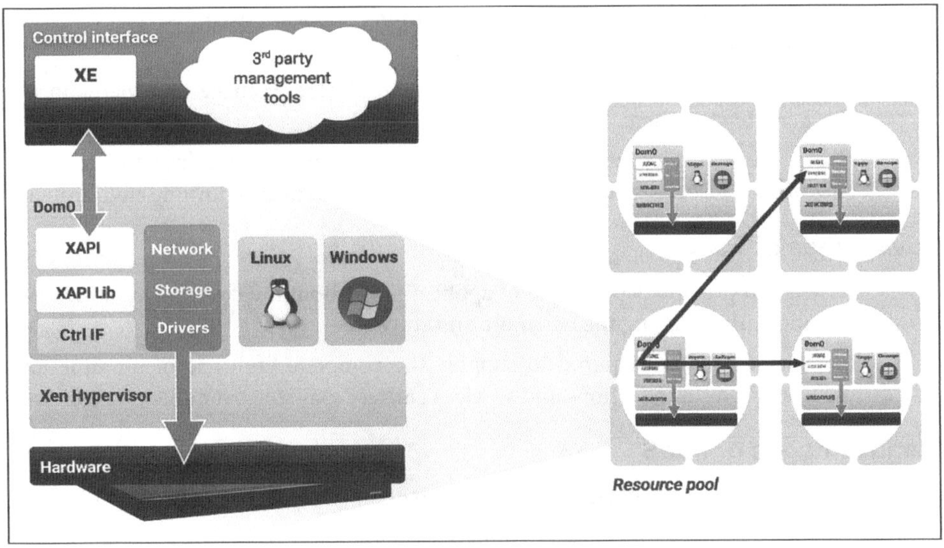

Fig. 2.6: Solution stack

2.2.1 PaaS Offers the Following

Facilities for application design Application development, Application testing, deployment Application services are,

- Operating system
- Server-side scripting environment
- Database Management system
- Server Software
- Support
- Storage
- Network access
- Tools for design and development
- Hosting

All these services may be provisioned as an integrated solution over the web.

2.2.2 Properties and Characteristics of PaaS

- Scalability
- Availability
- Manageability
- Performance
- Accessibility

2.2.3 PaaS Features

- It delivers the computing platform as service
- The capacities to abstract and control all the underlying resources It helps to providers any smallest unit of resources.

- To provide a reliable environment for running applications and services Act as a bridge between consumer and hardware.
- Do not need to care about how to build, configure, manage and maintain the backend environment.
- It provides a development and testing platform for running developed applications Reduce the responsibility of managing the development and runtime environment.

Advantages of PaaS

- It helps to provide deployment of application without the cost and complexity of buying and managing the hardware and software.
- It provides all the required to support the complete life cycle of building and delivering web applications and services entirely available from the internet.

Disadvantages of PaaS

- Less flexible than IaaS Dependency on provider.
- Adoption of software / system architecture required.

Evolving from different standards

Evolving "upwards" from IaaS:

- Amazon (Mail, Notification, Events, Databases, Workflow, etc.)

Evolving "downwards" from SaaS:

- Force.com – a place to host additional per-tenant logic. Google App Engine
- Evolving "sideways" from middleware platforms → WSO2, Tibco, vmWare, Oracle, IBM

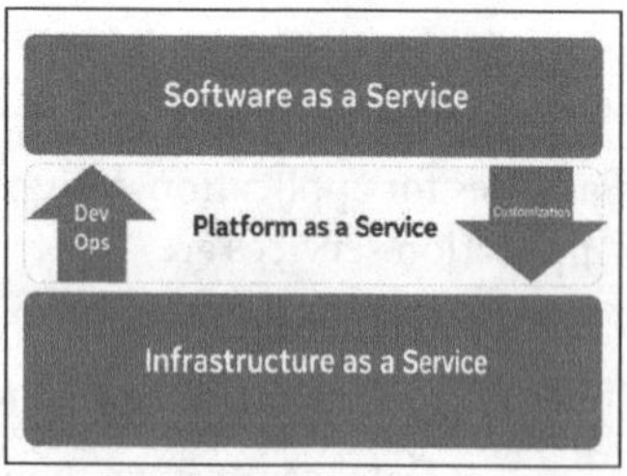

Fig. 2.7: SPI evolving standard

2.2.4 Generic PaaS Model

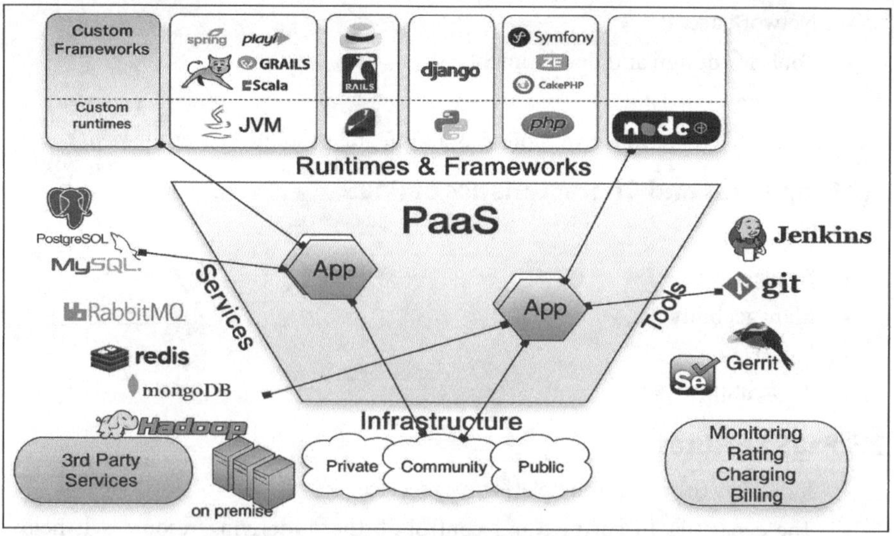

Fig. 2.8: General Paas Model

2.3 Infrastructure as a Service

This service offers the computing architecture and infrastructure i.e. all types of computing resources. All resources are offered in a virtual environment, so that multiple users can access it.

The resources are including such as Data storage, Virtualization Servers, Networking.

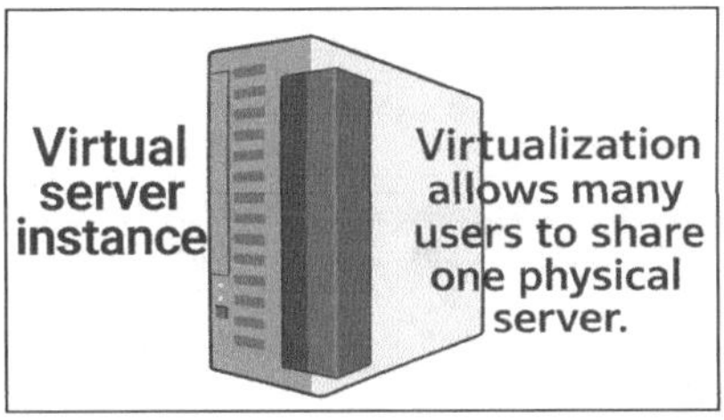

Fig. 2.9: IaaS and virtualization

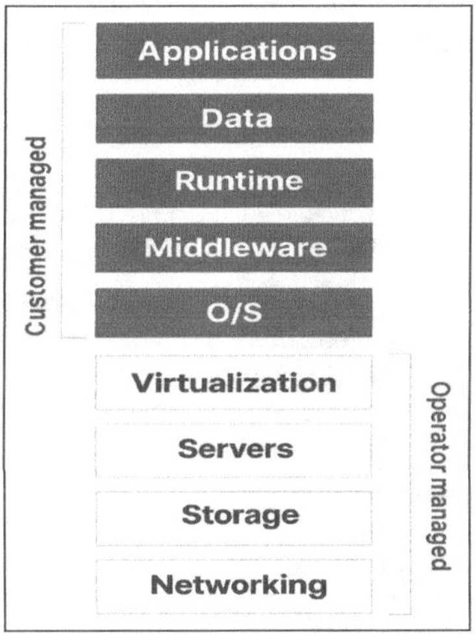

Fig. 2.10: IaaS architecture level

The vendors are responsible for managing all the computing resources which they provided. It allows existing applications to be run on a supplier's hardware.

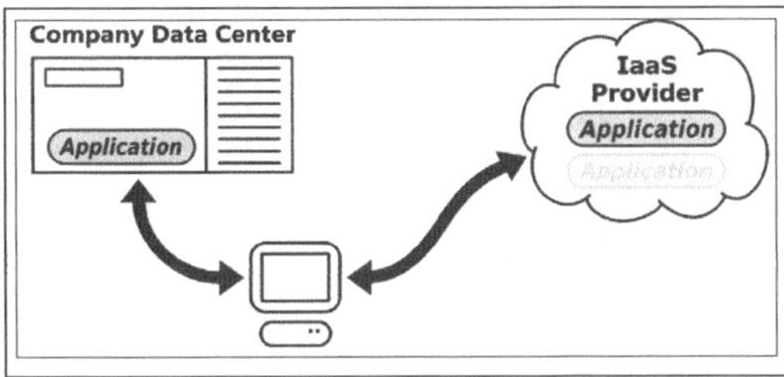

Fig. 2.11: User Task in IaaS Cloud

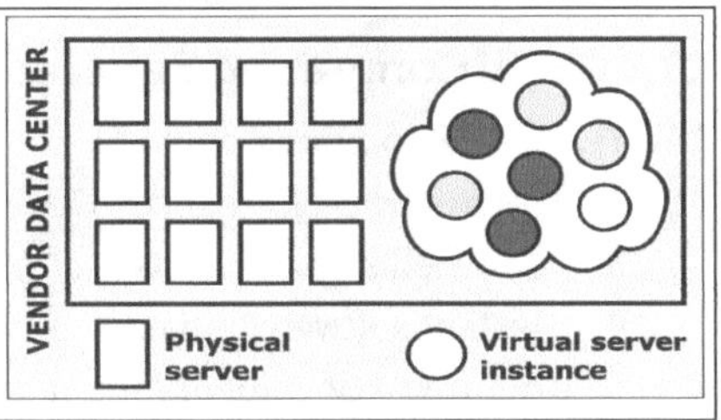

Fig. 2.12: Multiple user can access Virtual instances

The user responsible for handling other resources such as, Applications, Data Runtime and Middleware.

2.3.1 Example IaaS Service Providers

- AWS EC2 / S3 / RDS
- GoGrid
- RackSpace

Advantage of IaaS service providers

- The cloud provides the infrastructure
- Enhanced scalability i.e. dynamic workloads are supported It is flexible

Disadvantage of IaaS service providers

- Security issues
- Network and service delay

2.3.2 Comparison of Cloud Services

Blue indicates the levels owned and operated by the organization / Customer White levels are run and operated by the service provider / Operator

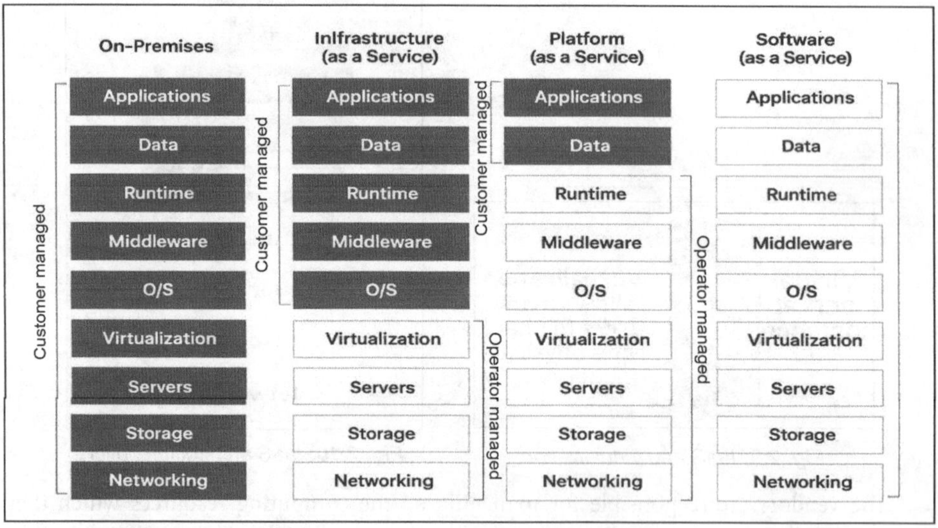

Fig. 2.13: Comparison of cloud services

2.3.3 Cloud Computing Services Pros

1. Lower computer costs
2. Improved performance:
3. Reduced software costs
4. Instant software updates
5. Improved document format compatibility
6. Unlimited storage capacity
7. Increased data reliability
8. Universal document access
9. Latest version availability
10. Easier group collaboration
11. Device independence

2.3.4 Cloud Computing Services Cons

1. Requires a constant Internet connection
2. Does not work well with low-speed connections
3. Features might be limited
4. Can be slow
5. Stored data can be lost
6. Stored data might not be secure

2.4 Web Services

Web services are XML-centered data exchange systems that use the internet for A2A (application-to-application) communication and interfacing. These processes involve programs, messages, documents, and/or objects.

Functions of Web Services

- Available over the internet or intranet networks
- Standardized XML messaging system
- Independent of a single operating system or programming language
- Self-describing via standard XML language
- Discoverable through a simple location method

Types of Web Services

XML-RPC (Remote Procedure Call) is the most basic XML protocol to exchange data between a wide variety of devices on a network. It uses HTTP to quickly and easily transfer data and communication other information from client to server.

- **UDDI** (Universal Description, Discovery, and Integration) is an XML-based standard for detailing, publishing, and discovering web services. It's basically an internet registry for businesses around the world. The goal is to streamline digital transactions and e-commerce among company systems.
- **SOAP**, is an XML-based Web service protocol to exchange data and documents over HTTP or SMTP (Simple Mail Transfer Protocol). It allows independent processes operating on disparate systems to communicate using XML.
- **REST**provides communication and connectivity between devices and the internet for API-based tasks. Most RESTful services use HTTP as the supporting protocol.

Web Services Which are Using Markup Languages

- Web template
- JSON-RPC
- JSON-WSP
- Web Services Description Language (WSDL)
- Web Services Conversation Language (WSCL)
- Web Services Flow Language (WSFL)
- Web Services Metadata Exchange (WS-MetadataExchange)
- XML Interface for Network Services (XINS)

WSDL

- WSDL stands for Web Services Description Language
- WSDL is used to describe web services
- WSDL is written in XML
- WSDL is a W3C recommendation from 26. June 2007

Table 1.2: WSDL Element and its description

WSDL Element Type	Description
<types>	Defines the (XML Schema) data types use by the web service
<message>	Defines the data elements for each operation
<portType>	Describes the operations that can be performed and the messages involved.
<binding>	Defines the protocol and data format f each port type

UDDI

UDDI is an XML-based standard for describing, publishing, and finding web services.

- UDDI stands for Universal Description, Discovery, and Integration.
- UDDI is a specification for a distributed registry of web services.
- UDDI is a platform-independent, open framework.
- UDDI can communicate via SOAP, CORBA, Java RMI Protocol.
- UDDI uses Web Service Definition Language(WSDL) to describe interfaces to web services.
- UDDI is seen with SOAP and WSDL as one of the three foundation standards of web services.
- UDDI is an open industry initiative, enabling businesses to discover each other and define how they interact over the Internet.

UDDI has two sections:

- A registry of all web service's metadata, including a pointer to the WSDL description of a service.
- A set of WSDL port type definitions for manipulating and searching that registry.

2.5 Service Oriented Architecture

Service

A service is a program we interact with via message exchanges A system is a set of deployed services cooperating in a given task.

Architecture

- Documentation organization Work breakdown structure Scheduling, planning, budgeting Unit testing, integration
- Architecture establishes the communication and coordination mechanisms among components

2.5.1 Software Architecture

It is collection of the fundamental decisions about a software product/solution designed to meet the project's quality attributes (i.e. requirements).The architecture includes the main components, their main attributes, and their collaboration (i.e. interactions and behavior) to meet the quality attributes.Architecture usually should be expressed in several levels of abstraction (depending on the project's size). Architecture is communicated from multiple viewpoints

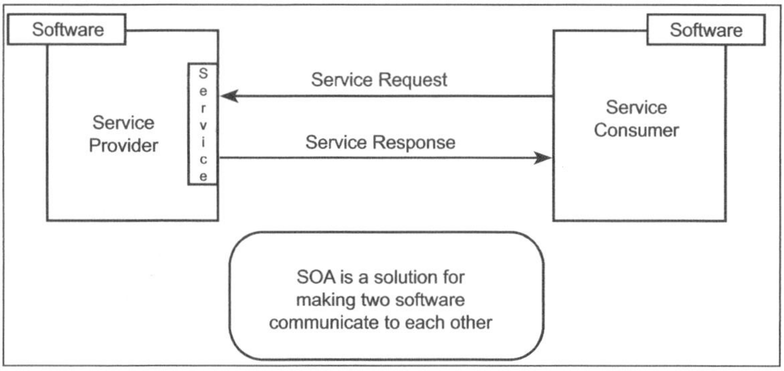

Fig. 2.14: SOA-Service Oriented Architecture

SOA

SOA stands for Service Oriented Architecture. It is a design pattern or software architecture which provides application functionality as a service to other applications. The basic principles of service-oriented architecture are independent of vendors, products and technologies. The services are provided to the other components through a communication protocol over a network. Every service has its own business logic.

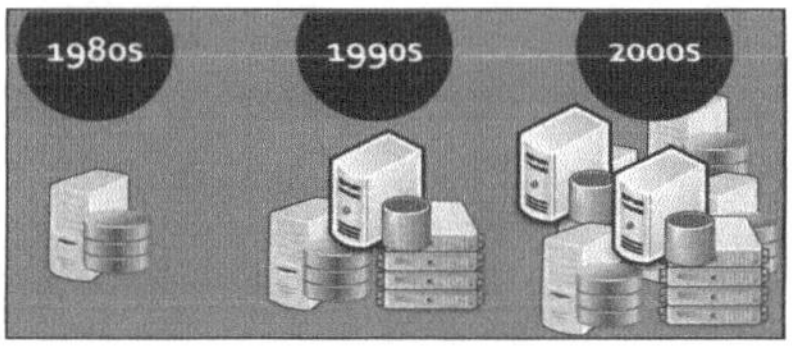

Fig. 2.15: Need for SOA

2.5.2 SOA Architecture

- **Consumer interface layer:** this layer is used by the customer.
- **Business process layer:** it provides the business process flow.
- **Service layer:** this layer comprises of all the services in the enterprises.
- **Component layerL:** this layer has the actual service to be provided.
- **Operational system layer:** this layer contains the data model.

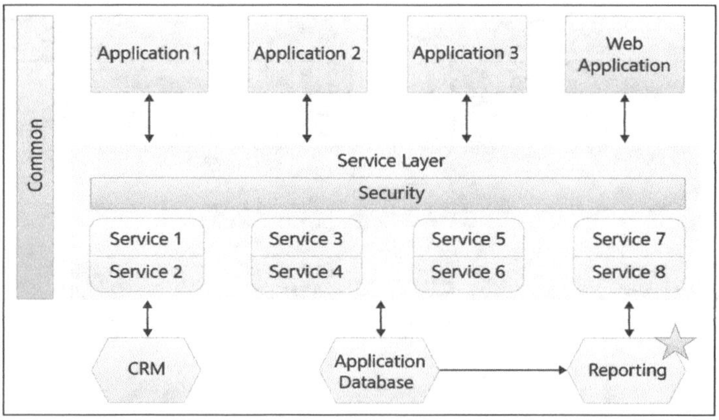

Fig. 2.16: Detailed SOA Architecture

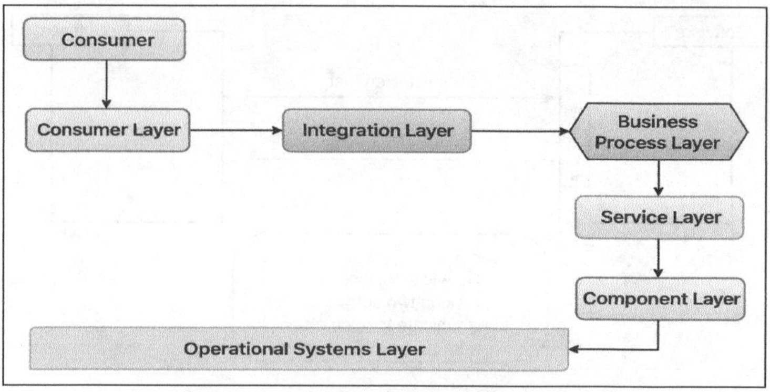

Fig. 2.17: SOA Architecture

Principles of SOA

a. **Service loose coupling:** service does not have high dependency implementation from outside world

b. **Service reusability:** services can be used again and again instead of rewriting them

c. **Service statelessness:** they usually do not maintain the state to reduce the resource consumption.

d. **Service discoverability:** services are registered in registry, so that the client can discover them in the service registry.

Applications

a. **Manufacturing:** E.g. Inventory management

b. **Insurance:** Take up the insurance of the employees in companies

Companies Using SOA

Banking Sector

a. ICICI Bank

b. HDFC Bank

c. UTI Bank etc.

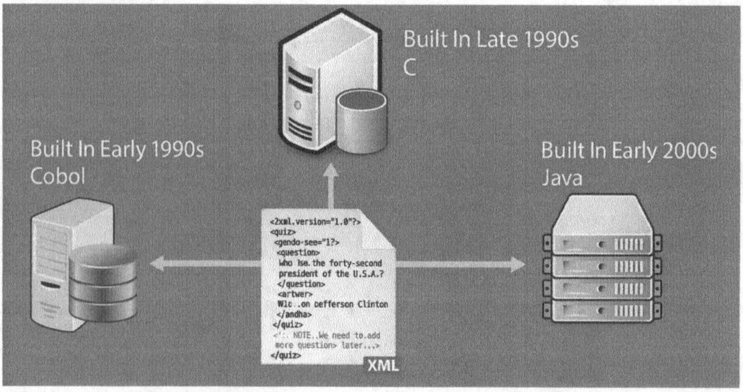

Fig. 2.18: Evolvement of SOA

Advantages of SOA

- Parallel application development
- Modular approach
- Easy maintenance
- Greater Reliability
- Improved Software Quality
- Platform Independence
- Increased Productivity

Disadvantages of SOA

- Stand alone, non-distributed applications
- Homogenous application environments
- GUI based applications
- Short lived applications
- Real time applications
- One-way asynchronous communication applications

2.5.3 Elastic Compute Cloud (EC2)

To access the **Elastic Compute Cloud (EC2)** functionality, access the **Amazon EC2** table inthe **AWS Console.**

Elastic Compute Cloud (EC2) is the engine room of AWS. This is where our servers will operate and run on a day-to-day basis. However, the 'elastic' in EC2 is there for a reason. EC2 is much more than just a bunch of servers! EC2 provides 'resizable compute capacity', or in other words can scale tremendously depending on our capacity requirements at a particular point in time. EC2 provides the ability to start and stop multiple servers from a single server image, as well as modifying the number of these instances dynamically. However, there have been some significant differences in the past on how this is implemented,which requires some up-front planning on how we will use the EC2 environment.

(i) General Roles of EC2 in the Architecture

EC2 is the backbone of the architecture where our servers are implemented. EC2 will not only run our servers but will manage the capacity that they produce.

Using EC2

To start using EC2 we must start with an EC2 'bundle' or Amazon Machine Image (AMI). Both Amazon and third parties such as Right Scale and IBM provide images. For this project, we will be using the default Windows Server Basic AMIs provided by AWS.

Each AMI is a starting point for our instance. Once we have started our Windows instance, we may need to wait up to 15 minutes for AWS to generate our password, so be patient, before wecan log on using Remote Desktop Protocol (RDP).Once our instance has started and we have RDP'd to it, we now have access to install any software that we need onto this instance. But beware, if we fail to create another bundle from our running instance—which we can use to start it next time—then all of our changes will be lost.

This is the major difference between standard instances in EC2 and the servers, which we havebeen familiar with up to now. When installing software onto a server that exists in our own server room, the software tends to remain installed. If we install software on an Amazon EC2 instance, our software (and data) will disappear when our instance is 'terminated'.

However, recently Amazon has introduced the concept of persistent EC2 images. These are AMIs, which are created on Elastic Block Store (EBS) disk. In this specific instance, changesmade to the image are persisted when we 'stop' the image. However, if we terminate the image,the changes are lost.

On Demand Computing

On-demand computing packages computer resources (processing, storage, and so forth) as a metered service similar to that of a public utility. In this model, customers pay for as much or as little processing and storage as they need. Companies that have large demand peaks followedby much lower normal usage periods particularly benefit from utility computing. The company pays more for their peak usage, of course, but their bills rapidly decline when the peak ends and normal usage patterns resume.

Clients of on-demand computing services essentially use these services as offsite virtual servers. Instead of investing in their own physical infrastructure, a company operates on a pay-as-we-go plan with a cloud services provider. On- demand computing itself is not a new concept, but has acquired new life thanks to cloud computing. In previous years, on-demand computing was provided from a single server via some sort of time-sharing arrangement. Today, the service is based on large grids of computers operating as a single cloud.

2.6 Cloud Service Management

The management of cloud infrastructure products and services is cloud management. Public clouds are operated by public cloud service providers, which provide the servers, storage, networking and data centre operations of the public cloud environment. With a third-party cloud management tool, users can also choose to manage their public cloud services. Public cloud service users can typically choose from three categories of specific cloud provisioning:

- **User self-provisioning:** Users, usually via a web form or console interface, buy cloud services directly from the provider. On a per-transaction basis, the client pays.
- **Advanced provisioning:** A pre-determined sum of services scheduled in advance of operation is contracted in advance by customers. A flat fee or a monthly fee is charged by the consumer.
- **Dynamic provisioning:** When the client requires them, the provider allocates resources, and then decommissions them when they are no longer required. On a pay- per-use basis, the client is paid.

The purpose and scope of the management of cloud services are listed below:

- **Purpose:** Establish suitable techniques for managing and running cloud-based services. Insert cloud service management techniques into current frameworks for IT creation and support.

- **Scope:** Oversight of cloud-based service design, development and change. Cloud-based service management and operation.

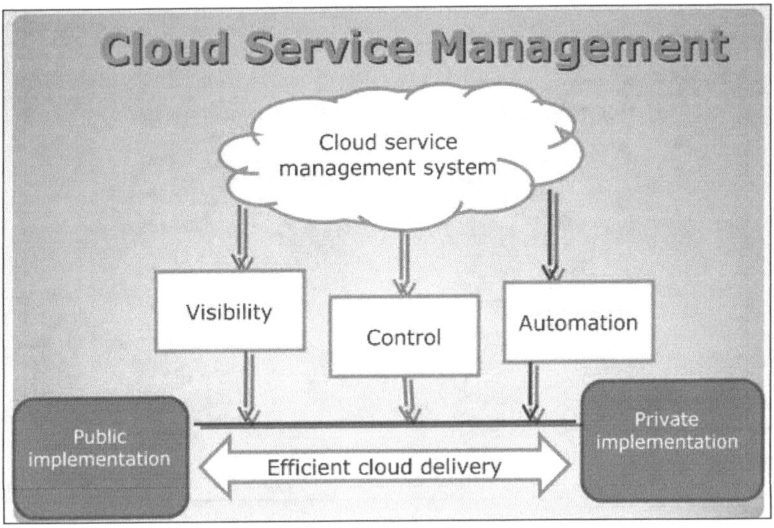

Fig. 2.19: *Cloud Service Management*

Characteristics of Cloud Service Management

In a design for handling cloud environments, cloud management incorporates applications and technologies. With a range of cloud management platforms and instruments, software developers have responded to the management challenges of cloud computing. These solutions include native tools provided by public cloud providers, as well as third-party tools designed by various cloud providers to provide consistent functionality. With access to various native features within individual cloud platforms, administrators must balance the conflicting requirements of efficient consistency across various cloud platforms. The need for transparent cross-platform management is motivated by increasing public cloud adoption and increased multi- cloud use. For those technical professionals responsible for maintaining IT systems

2.7 Multitenancy

In cloud computing, multitenancy means that multiple customers of a cloud vendor are using the same computing resources. Despite the fact that they share resources, cloud customers aren't aware of each other, and their data is kept totally separate. Multitenancy is a crucial component of cloud computing; without it, cloud services would be far less practical. Multitenant architecture is a feature in many types of public cloud computing, including IaaS, PaaS, SaaS, containers, and serverless computing.

To understand multitenancy, think of how banking works. Multiple people can store their money in one bank, and their assets are completely separate even though they're stored in the same place. Customers of the bank don't interact with each other, don't have access to other customers' money, and aren't even aware of each other. Similarly, in public cloud computing, customers of the cloud vendor use the same infrastructure – the same servers, typically – while still keeping their data and their business logic separate and secure.

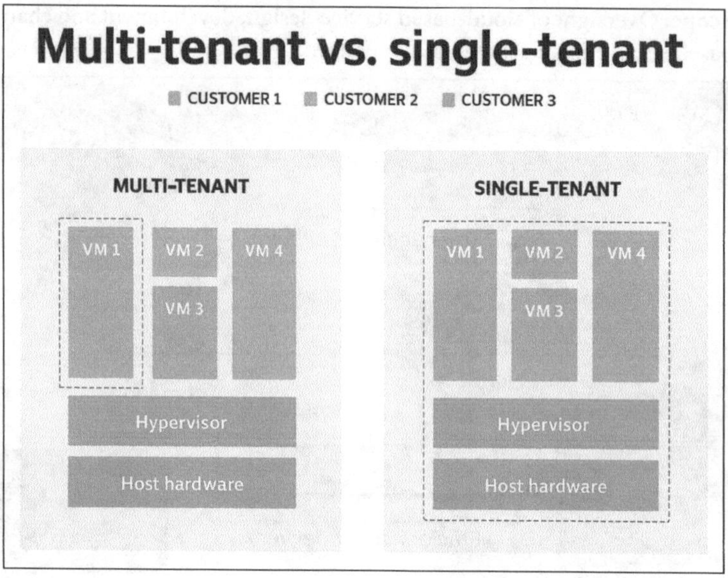

(a)

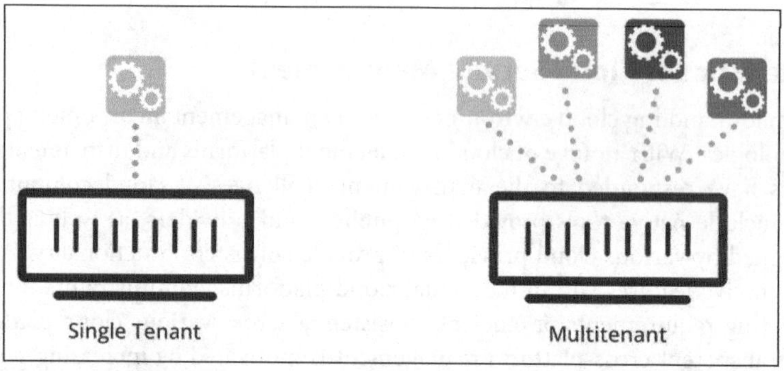

(b)

***Fig. 2.20:** (a) Single and multitenant architectures (b) Single and multitenant architectures*

The classic definition of multitenancy was a single software instance* that served multiple users, or tenants. However, in modern cloud computing, the term has taken on a broader meaning, referring to shared cloud infrastructure instead of just a shared software instance.

A software instance is a copy of a running program loaded into random access memory (RAM).

1. Multitenancy and Cloud Computing

In cloud computing, applications and data are hosted in remote servers in various data centers and accessed over the Internet. Data and applications are centralized in the cloud instead of being located on individual client devices (like laptops or smartphones) or in servers within a company's offices.Many modern applications are cloud-based, which is why, for example, a user can access their Facebook account and upload content from multiple devices.

2. Benefits of Multitenancy

Many of the benefits of cloud computing are only possible because of multitenancy. Here are two crucial ways multitenancy improves cloud computing:

- **Better use of resources:** One machine reserved for one tenant isn't efficient, as that one tenant is not likely to use all of the machine's computing power. By sharing machines among multiple tenants, use of available resources is maximized.
- **Lower costs:** With multiple customers sharing resources, a cloud vendor can offer their services to many customers at a much lower cost than if each customer required their own dedicated infrastructure.

3. Drawbacks of Multitenancy

Possible security risks and compliance issues: Some companies may not be able to store data within shared infrastructure, no matter how secure, due to regulatory requirements. Additionally, security problems or corrupted data from one tenant could spread to other tenants on the same machine, although this is extremely rare and shouldn't occur if the cloud vendor has configured their infrastructure correctly. These security risks are somewhat mitigated by the fact that cloud vendors typically are able to invest more in their security than individual businesses can.

The "noisy neighbor" effect: If one tenant is using an inordinate amount of computing power, this could slow down performance for the other tenants. Again, this should not occur if the cloud vendor has set up their infrastructure correctly.

Case Study on Cloudfare Solutions to Support Multitenancy in Different Categories

a. Mutlitenancy Support in Public Cloud Computing

Imagine a special car engine that could be shared easily between multiple cars and car owners. Each car owner needs the engine to behave slightly differently: some car owners require a powerful 8-cylinder engine, while others require a more fuel- efficient 4-cylinder engine. Now imagine that this special engine is able to morph itself each time it starts up so that it can better meet the car owner's needs.

This is similar to the way many public cloud providers implement multitenancy. Most cloud providers define multitenancy as a shared software instance. They store metadata* about each tenant and use this data to alter the software instance at runtime to fit each tenant's needs. The tenants are isolated from each other via permissions. Even though they all share the same software instance, they each use and experience the software differently.

b. Multitenancy Support in Container Architecture

Containers are self-contained bundles of software that include an application, system libraries, system settings, and everything else the application needs in order to run. Containers help ensure that an application runs the same no matter where it is hosted.

Containers are partitioned from each other into different user space environments, and each container runs as if it were the only system on that host machine. Because containers are self-contained, multiple containers created by different cloud customers can run on a single host machine.

c. Multitenancy Support in Serverless Computing

Serverless computing is a model in which applications are broken up into smaller pieces called functions, and each function only runs on demand, separately from the other functions. (This model of cloud computing is also known as Function-as-a-Service, or FaaS.)

As the name implies, serverless functions do not run on dedicated servers, but rather on any available machine in the serverless provider's infrastructure. Because companies are not assigned their own discrete physical servers, serverless providers will often be running code from several of their customers on a single server at any given time – another example of multitenancy.

Some serverless platforms use Node.js for executing serverless code. The Cloudflare serverless platform, Cloudflare Workers, uses Chrome V8, in which each function runs in its own sandbox, or separate environment. This keeps serverless functions totally separate from each other even when they're running on the same infrastructure.

d. Multitenancy Support in Private Cloud Computing

Private cloud computing uses multitenant architecture in much the same way that public cloud computing does. The difference is that the other tenants are not from external organizations. In public cloud computing, Company A shares infrastructure with Company B. In private cloud computing, different teams within Company A share infrastructure with each other.

Multitenant Cloud Architecture

A **multitenant cloud architecture** describes a single cloud instance and infrastructure purpose-built to support multiple customers.

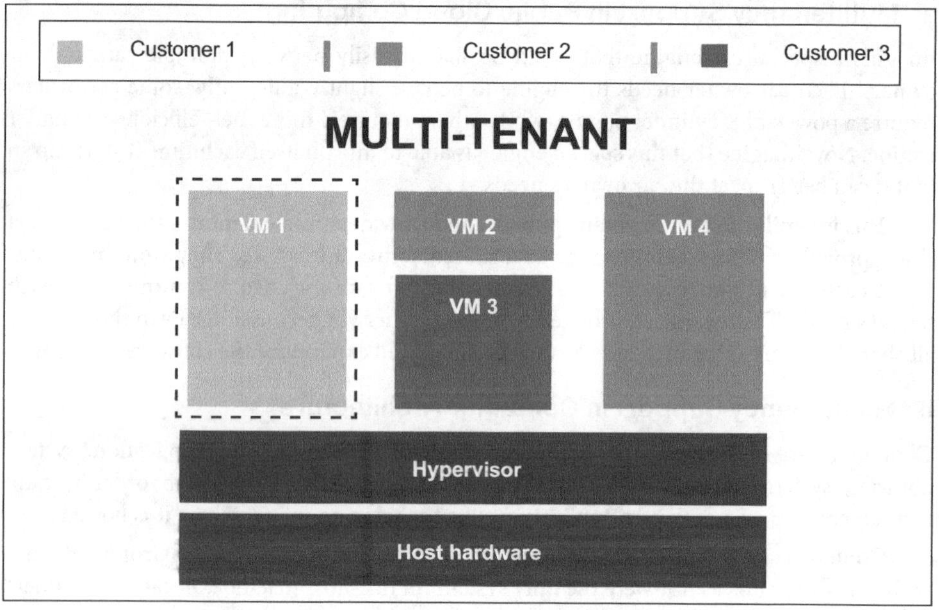

Fig. 2.21: Multitenant architecture

Multitenancy can describe hardware or software architectures in which multiple systems, applications, or data from different enterprises are hosted on the same physical hardware. This differs from single-tenancy, in which a server runs one instance of an operating system and application. In the cloud world, a multitenant cloud architecture enables customers ("tenants") to share computing resources in a public or private cloud. Multitenancy is a common feature of purpose-built, cloud- delivered services, as it allows customers to share resources efficiently while securely scaling to meet increasing demand. Despite the fact that they share resources, cloud customers aren't aware of each other and their data is kept totally separate.

EXERCISE

A. Objective Questions

1. Explains the Web Services and role of web services in SOA.
2. Eloborate the Service Oriented Architecture
3. Describe the Cloud Service Management and Multitentancy, Single tentancy
4. What are the three main cloud service models? Explain each with examples.
5. Compare and contrast SaaS, PaaS, and IaaS in terms of their advantages and use cases.
6. Discuss the advantages and disadvantages of using PaaS for application development.
7. What are the security challenges associated with PaaS?
8. What are the key components of IaaS, and how do they benefit enterprises?
9. Explain the role of virtualization in IaaS.
10. What are the benefits and challenges of implementing SOA in cloud computing?
11. Explain the role of web services in SOA.
12. Compare multitenancy with single-tenancy in cloud computing.
13. What is cloud service management, and why is it important?

B. Objective Questions

1. Which of the following is NOT a cloud service model?
   (a) SaaS (b) PaaS
   (c) IaaS (d) DaaS
2. hich of the following is an example of PaaS?
   (a) Google Docs (b) AWS EC2
   (c) Microsoft Azure App Service (d) Dropbox
3. What is a key advantage of PaaS?
   (a) Provides complete control over hardware resources
   (b) Offers a platform for developing applications without managing the infrastructure
   (c) Requires users to handle software installation and updates
   (d) Only supports private cloud environments

4. Which cloud model provides virtualized computing resources like storage, networking, and servers?
   (a) SaaS (b) PaaS
   (c) IaaS (d) DaaS
5. What is the main benefit of IaaS?
   (a) Users do not need to manage underlying hardware
   (b) Users have to handle application development and hosting
   (c) It only supports web applications
   (d) Provides limited scalability
6. What is a web service in cloud computing?
   (a) A local application running on a private network
   (b) A software system designed to support machine-to-machine interaction over a network
   (c) A physical cloud storage device
   (d) A database management system
7. Which protocol is commonly used for web services?
   (a) HTTP (b) SMTP
   (c) FTP (d) POP3
8. Which of the following is an example of a web service?
   (a) Google Docs (b) Amazon S3
   (c) REST API (d) Microsoft Excel
9. Which architecture is SOA closely associated with?
   (a) Microservices (b) Monolithic applications
   (c) Mainframe computing (d) Desktop applications
10. hat is multitenancy in cloud computing?
    (a) A cloud model that provides multiple backup options
    (b) A software architecture where multiple customers share a single instance of software and infrastructure
    (c) A dedicated cloud infrastructure for one organization
    (d) A cloud computing model for personal users only

UNIT 3

Cloud Deployment Models and Virtualization

3.1 Deployment Models

A deployment model defines the purpose of the cloud and the nature of how the cloud is located. The NIST definition for the four deployment models is as follows:

- **Public cloud:** The public cloud infrastructure is available for public use alternatively for a large industry group and is owned by an organization selling cloud services.
- **Private cloud:** The private cloud infrastructure is operated for the exclusive use of an organization. The cloud may be managed by that organization or a third party. Private cloudsmay be either on- or off-premises.
- **Hybrid cloud:** A hybrid cloud combines multiple clouds (private, community of public) where those clouds retain their unique identities, but are bound together as a unit. A hybrid cloud may offer standardized or proprietary access to data and applications, as well as application portability.
- **Community cloud:** A community cloud is one where the cloud has been organized toserve a common function or purpose. It may be for one organization or for several organizations, but they share common concerns such as their mission, policies, security, regulatory compliance needs, and so on. Acommunity cloud may be managed by the constituent organization(s) or by a third party.

The following figure shows the different locations that clouds can come in. In the sections that follow, these different cloud deployment models are described in more detail.

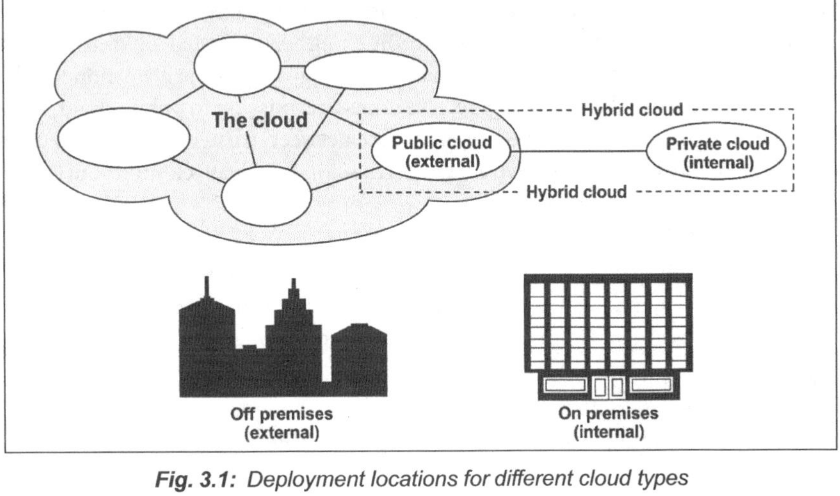

Fig. 3.1: Deployment locations for different cloud types

3.2 Cloud Deployment of Applications on the Cloud

3.2.1 Deployment to the Cloud

Cloud deployment refers to the enablement of SaaS (software as a service), PaaS (platform as a service) or IaaS (infrastructure as a service) solutions that may be accessed on demand by end users or consumers. A cloud deployment model refers to the type of cloud computing architecture a cloud solution will be implemented on. Cloud deployment includes all of the required installation and configuration steps that must be implemented before user provisioning can occur.

3.2.2 SAAS Deployment & Cloud Deployment Models

Cloud deployment can be viewed from the angle of management responsibility for the deployment of the SaaS, PaaS and/or IaaS solutions in question. From this perspective, there are two possible approaches: the cloud solution(s) may be deployed by a third party (under a community cloud, public cloud or private cloud deployment model) or the cloud solution(s) may be deployed by a single entity (under a private cloud deployment model).

SaaS deployment is a type of cloud deployment that is typically initiated using a public cloud or a private cloud deployment model, however SaaS deployment may also be initiated using a hybrid cloud deployment model, when hybrid cloud resources are owned and/or managed by the same entity. Expanding on this theme is the existence of virtual private clouds that can be used for SaaSdeployment as well. Virtual private clouds are technically public clouds that function the same asprivate clouds, since only trusted entities may gain access to the virtual private cloud resources.

Regardless of whether or not a SaaS solution is deployed in a public cloud, a private cloud, a virtual private cloud or a hybrid cloud; many SaaS solutions provide automatic deployment for the cloud services being delivered. SaaS deployment provides many additional benefits over the traditional model of software deployment, including scalability, where application users can be added or subtracted on demand without concerns over capital investments in additional hardwareor software. SaaS deployment also provides above average up-time for enterprise applications as compared to on premise software deployment.

After cloud deployment has been completed for a SaaS, PaaS or IaaS solution, user provisioning can occur based on user permissions, where access is provided for cloud resources based on the consumer's classification as either a trusted or untrusted entity. Trusted entities may receive accesspermission to managed cloud, private cloud or hybrid cloud resources. Untrusted entities may receive access permission to public cloud, managed cloud or hybrid cloud resources. The key difference between trusted and untrusted entities is that untrusted entities never receive access permission to private cloud resources.

3.2.3 Cloud Data Centers

A data center is a facility that centralizes an organization's IT operations and equipment, as well as where it stores, manages, and disseminates its data. Data centers house a network's most critical systems and are vital to the continuity of daily operations.

The term "data center" can be interpreted in a few different ways. First, an organization can run an in-house data center maintained by trained IT employees whose job it is to keep the system up and running. Second, it can refer to an offsite storage center that consists of servers and other equipment needed to keep the stored data accessible both virtually and physically.

Pros: Data centers come with a number of pros. Organizations able to have an in-house data storage center are far less reliant on maintaining an Internet connection. Data will be accessible as long as the local network remains stable. Remote storage has its advantages as well. If the organization's locationis compromised via fire, break-in, flooding, etc., the data will remain untouched and unharmed at its remote location.

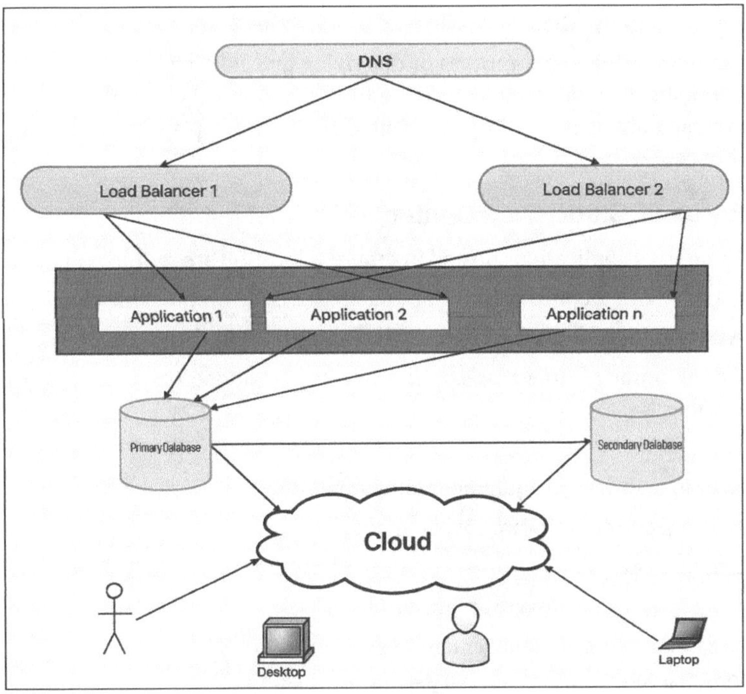

***Fig. 3.2:** Cloud Data Center Architecture*

Cons: Having all or most of our data stored in one location makes it more easily accessible to those we don't want having access, both virtually and physically. Depending on our organization's budget, it could prove too expensive to maintain an organization-owned and operated data center. A data center is ideal for companies that need a customized, dedicated system that gives them full control over their data and equipment. Since only the company will be using the infrastructure's poor,a data center is also more suitable for organizations that run many different types of applications and complex workloads. A data center, however, has limited capacity -- once we build a data center, we will not be able to change the amount of storage and workload it can withstand without purchasing andinstalling more equipment.

On the other hand, a cloud system is scalable to our business needs. It has potentially unlimited capacity, based on our vendor's offerings and service plans. One disadvantage of the cloud is that we will not have as much control as we would a data center, since a third party is managing the system. Furthermore, unless we have a private cloud within the company network, we will be sharing resourceswith other cloud users in our provider's public cloud.

3.2.4 Difference Between a Data Center and Cloud Computing

The main difference between a cloud and a data center is that a cloud is an off-premise form of computing that stores data on the Internet, whereas a data center refers to on-premise hardware thatstores data within an organization's local network. Where is data stored in the cloud?

Cloud storage is a model of data storage in which the digital data is stored in logical pools, the physical storage spans multiple servers (and often locations), and the physical environment is typicallyowned and managed by a hosting company.

Data center hosting is the process of deploying and hosting a data center on a third-party or externalservice provider's infrastructure. It enables the use of the same services, features and capabilities of a data center but from a hosted platform external to the on-premises data center or IT infrastructure.

Key Features of Cloud Data Center

- Number of applications hosted in different location are residing on the same cloud
- Primary and secondary (back up) database reside on the same cloud
- As secondary database resides on the same cloud so there wouldbe no loss of data.
- At any point of time new applications can be added on cloud, since it is easily scalable.
- Stores data on the Internet
- Requires no special equipment and knowledge
- Homogeneous hardware environment
- Simple workloads
- Single standard software architecture
- Uses standardized management tools
- The cost of running cloud data center is much low
- Cloud data center is an external form of computing so it may be less secure.
- Self-service, pay per use
- Automated recovery in case of failure
- Renting is on basis of logical usage
- Platform Independent
- Easily scalable on demand

With passing years the transaction of data across the network is going to boom and thereby the needof storage is going to increase rapidly. When thinking about management of such rapidly growing data chain, data center will soon lose its dominant status. The reason behind this is scalability and the operating cost of data center. Traditional data centers are heavily bound by physical limitations, making expansion a major concern. Even if data center manages the explosion of data still no company would afford to buy it. Due to energy cost involved in running and cooling the data center,life of traditional data center is soon to end. And as a result, Cloud data center would be replacing traditional data center. Cloud data center can operate with bulk of data being generated. Due to its pay-as-we-use model, companies find it more reliable to work with. Minimal cost is required for operating cloud which again wins over traditional data center. The results clearly state that Cloud data center offers immense potential in areas of scale, cost, and maintenance.

3.2.5 Energy Efficiency in Data Center

Cloud computing is an internet based computing which provides metering based services to consumers. It means accessing data from a centralized pool of compute resources that can be ordered and consumedon demand. It also provides computing resources through virtualization over internet.

Data center is the most prominent in cloud computing which contains collection of servers on which Business information is stored and applications run. Data center which includes servers, cables, air conditioner, network etc.. consumes more poour and releases huge amount of Carbon-di-oxide (CO_2) to the environment. One of the most important challenge faced in cloud computing is the optimizationof Energy Utilization. Hence the concept of green cloud computing came into existence.

There are multiple techniques and algorithms used to minimize the energy consumption in cloud.

Techniques include:

1. Dynamic Voltage and Frequency Scaling (DVFS)
2. Virtual Machine (VM)
3. Migration and VM Consolidation

Algorithms are:

1. Maximum Bin Packing
2. Poour Expand Min-Max and Minimization Migrations
3. Highest Potential growth

The main purpose of all these approaches is to optimize the energy utilization in cloud.

Cloud Computing as per NIST is, "Cloud Computing is a model for enabling ubiquitous, convenient, on-demand network access to a shared pool of configurable computing resources (e.g., networks, servers, storage, applications and services) that can be rapidly provisioned and released with minimal management effort or service provider interaction." Now-a-days most of the business enterprises and individual IT Companies are opting for cloud in order to share business information.

The main expectation of cloud service consumer is to have a reliable service. To satisfy consumer's expectation several Data centers are established all over the world and each Data center contains thousands of servers. Small amount of workload on server consumes 50% of the poour supply..Cloudservice providers ensure that reliable and load balancing services to the consumers around the world bykeeping servers ON all the time. To satisfy this SLA provider has to supply poour continuously to datacenters leads to huge amount of energy utilization by the data center and simultaneously increases the cost of investment.

The major challenge is utilization of energy efficiently and hence develops an eco-friendly cloud computing.

The idle servers and resources in data center wastes huge amount of energy. Energy also wasted whenthe server is overloaded. Few techniques such as load balancing, VM virtualization, VM migration, resource allocation and job scheduling etc. are used to solve the problem. It is alsomfound that transporting data between data centers and home computers can consume even larger amounts of energy than storing it.

3.2.6 Green Computing

Green computing is the Eco-friendly use of computers and their resources. It is also defined as the study and practice of designing, engineering, manufacturing and disposing computing resources with minimal environmental damage.

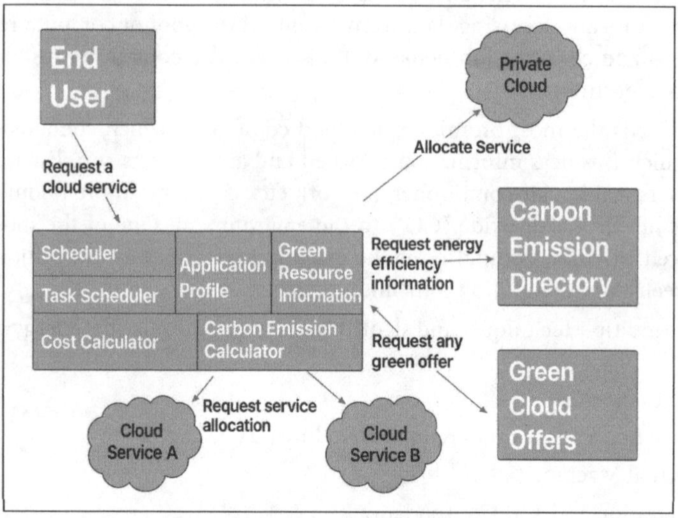

Fig. 3.3: Green Cloud Architecture

Green cloud computing is using Internet computing services from a service provider that has taken measures to reduce their environmental effect and also green cloud computing is cloud computing with-less environmental impact.

Some measures taken by the Internet service providers to make their services greener are:

1. Use renewable energy sources.
2. Make the data center more energy efficient, for example by maximizing power usage efficiency(PUE).
3. Reuse waste heat from computer servers (e.g. to heat nearby buildings).
4. Make sure that all hardware is properly recycled at the end of its life.
5. Use hardware that has a long lifespan and contains little to no toxic materials.

3.2.7. Mobile Cloud Computing Service Models

Mobile cloud computing (MCC) is a technique or model, in which mobile applications are built, poured and hosted using cloud computing technology. MCC is used to bring benefits for mobile users,network operators, as well as cloud providers. Compact design, high quality graphics, customized user applications support and multi-modal connectivity features have made Static Memory Deduplication (SMD) a special choice of interest for mobile users. SMDs incorporate the computing potentials of PDAs and voice communication capabilities of ordinary mobile devices by providing support for customized user applications and multi-modal connectivity for accessing both cellular and data networks. SMDs are the dominant future computing devices with high user expectations for accessing computational intensive applications analogous to poourful stationary computing machines.

A key area of mobile computing research focuses on the application layer research for creating new software level solutions. Application offloading is an application layer solution for alleviating resources limitations in SMDs. Successful practices of cloud computing for stationary machines are the motivating factors for leveraging cloud resources and services for SMDs. Cloud computing employs different services provision models for the provision of cloud resources and services to SMDs; such as Software as a Service, Infrastructure as a Service, and Platform as a Service. Several online file storage services are available on cloud server for augmenting storage potentials of client devices; such as Amazon S3, Google Docs, MobileMe, and DropBox. In the same way, Amazon provides cloud computing services- in the form of Elastic Cloud Compute. The cloud revolution augments the computing potentials of client devices; such as desktops, laptops, PDAs and smart phones.

The aim of MCC is to alleviate resources limitations of SMDs by leveraging computing resources and services of cloud datacenters. MCC is deployed in diverse manners to achieve the aforementioned objective. MCC employs process offloading techniques for augmenting application processing potentials of SMDs. In application offloading intensive applications are offloaded to remote server nodes. Current offloading procedures employ diverse strategies for the deployment of runtime distributed application processing platform on SMDs.

The term "Mobile Cloud Computing" was introduced no longer after the introduction of "Cloud Computing". It has been a major attraction as it offers reduced development and running cost. Definitions of Mobile Cloud Computing can be classified into two classes; first one refers to carrying out data storages and processing outside the mobile device i.e on cloud. Here mobile devices simply acts as a terminal, only intended to provide an easy convenient way of accessing service in cloud. Thebenefit of this is that the main obstacle of mobile low storage and processing poour are avoided and level of security is provided via acute security applications.

The second definition refers to computing where data storage and computing are carried out on mobiledevice. Using mobile hardware for cloud computing has advantages over using traditional hardware. These advantages include computational access to multimedia and sensor data without the need for large network transfers, more efficient access to data stored on other mobile devices, and distributed ownership and maintenance of hardware. Using these definition one can clarify the differences betweenmobile computing and cloud computing. Cloud computing aims at providing service without the knowledge of end user of where these services are hosted or how they are delivered. Whereas Mobile computing aims to provide mobility so, that users can access resources through wireless technology from anywhere.

Mobile cloud computing is the latest practical computing paradigm that extends utility computing vision of computational clouds to resources constrained SMDs. MCC is defined as a new distributed computing paradigm for mobile applications whereby the storage and the data processing are migratedfrom the SMD to resources rich and powerful centralized computing data centers in computational clouds.

The centralized applications, services and resources are accessed over the wireless network technologies based on web browser on the SMDs. Successful practice of accessing computational clouds on demand for stationary computers motivate for leveraging cloud services and resources for SMDs. MCC has been attracting the attentions of businesspersons as a profitable business option that reduces the development and execution cost of mobile applications and mobile users are enabled to acquire new technology conveniently on demand basis. MCC enables to achieve rich experience of a variety of cloud services for SMD at low cost on the move. MCC prolongs diverse services models ofcomputational clouds for mitigating computing resources (battery, CPU, memory) limitations in SMDs.

The objective of MCC is to augment computing potentials of SMDs by employing resources and services of computational clouds. MCC focuses on alleviating resources limitations in SMDs by employing different augmentation strategies; such as screen augmentation, energy augmentation, storage augmentation and application processing augmentation of SMD.A taxonomy including three main approaches have been devised, namely high-end resource production, native resource conservation, and resource requirement reduction has been analyzed. MCC utilizes cloud storage services for providing online storage and cloud processing services for augmenting processing capabilities of SMDs. Processing capabilities of SMDs are augmented by outsourcing computational intensive components of the mobile applications to cloud datacenters. The following section discussesthe concept of augmenting smartphones through computational clouds.

3.2.8 Augmenting Smartphones Through Computational Clouds

MCC implements a number of augmentation procedures for leveraging resources and services of cloud datacenters. Examples of the augmentations strategies include; screen augmentation, energy augmentation, storage augmentation and application processing augmentation of SMD. In MCC, twocategories of the cloud services are of special interest to research community; cloud contents and computing power. Cloud contents are provided in the form of centralized storage centers or sharing online contents such as live video streams from other mobile devices.

A number of online file storageservices are available on cloud server which augments the storage potentials by providing off-device storage services. Examples of the cloud storage services include Amazon S3 and DropBox. Mobile users outsource data storage by maintaining data storage on cloud server nodes. However, ensuring theconsistency of data on the cloud server nodes and mobile devices is still a challenging research perspective.

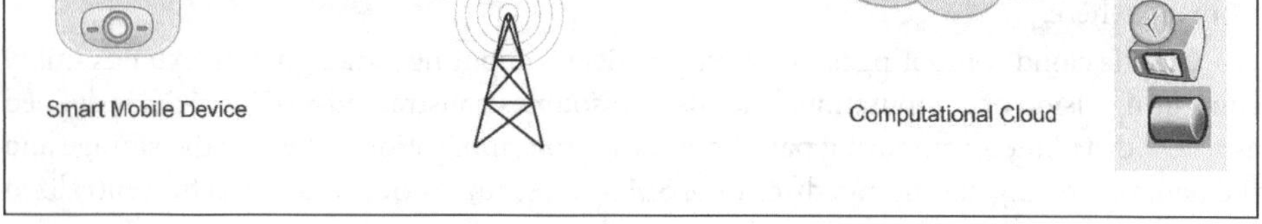

Fig. 3.4: Mobile users outsource data storage

Mobile Cloud Computing Model SmartBox is an online file storage and management model whichprovides a constructive approach for online cloud based storage and access management system. Similarly, the computing poour of the cloud datacenters is utilized by outsourcing computational loadto cloud server nodes. The mechanism of outsourcing computational task to remote server is called process offloading or cyber foraging. Smart mobile devices implement process offloading to utilize thecomputing poour of the cloud. The term cyber foraging is introduced to augment the computing potentials of wireless mobile devices by exploiting available stationary computers in the local environment.

The mechanism of outsourcing computational load to remote surrogates in the close proximity is called cyber foraging. Researchers extend process offloading algorithms for Pervasive Computing, Grid Computing and Cluster Computing. In recent years, a number of cloud server based application offloading frameworks are introduced for outsourcing computational intensive componentsof the mobile applications partially or entirely to cloud datacenters. Mobile applications which are attributed with the features of runtime partitioning are called elastic mobile applications. Elastic applications are partitioned at runtime for the establishment of distributed processing platform.

3.3 Need for virtualization

Virtualization is the ability which allows sharing the physical instance of a single application or resource among multiple organizations or users. This technique is done by assigning a name logically to all those physical resources & provides a pointer to those physical resources based on demand.

Over an existing operating system & hardware, we generally create a virtual machine which and aboveit we run other operating systems or applications. This is called Hardware Virtualization. The virtual machine provides a separate environment that is logically distinct from its underlying hardware. Here,the system or the machine is the host & virtual machine is the guest machine. This virtual environmentis managed by a firmware which is termed as a hypervisor.

Virtualization plays a significant role in cloud technology and its working mechanism. Usually, what happens in the cloud - the users not only share the data that are located in the cloud like an applicationbut also share their infrastructures with the help of virtualization. Virtualization is used mainly to provide applications with standard versions for the cloud customers & with the release of the latest version of an application the providers can efficiently provide that application to the cloud and its users and it is possible using virtualization only. By the use of this virtualization concept, all servers & software other cloud providers require those are maintained by a third-party, and the cloud provider pays them on a monthly or yearly basis. In reality, most of the today's hypervisor make use of a combination of different types of hardware virtualization. Mainly virtualization means running multiple systems on a single machine but sharing all resources (hardware) & it helps to share IT resources to get benefit in the business field.

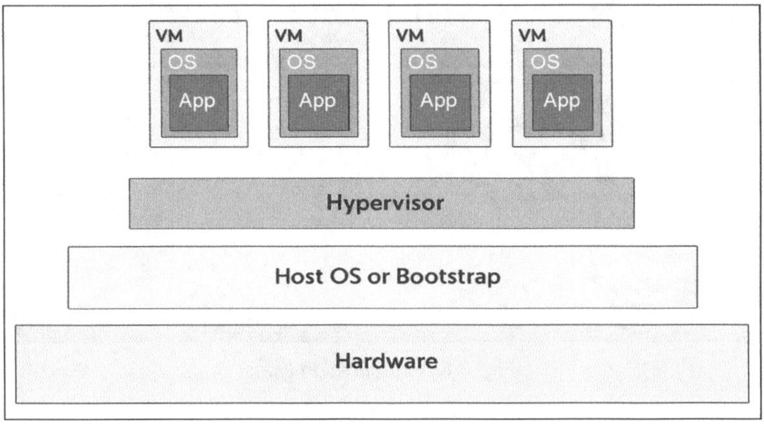

Fig. 3.5: Cloud Virtualization

3.3.1 Difference Between Virtualization and Cloud

1. Essentially there is a gap between these two terms, though cloud technology requires the concept of virtualization. Virtualization is a technology - it can also be treated as software that can manipulate hardware. Whereas cloud computing is a service which is the result of the manipulation.
2. Virtualization is the foundation element of cloud computing whereas Cloud technology is the deliveryof shared resources as a service-on-demand via the internet.
3. Cloud is essentially made-up from the concept of virtualization.

3.3.2 Advantages of Virtualization

- The number of servers gets reduced by the use of virtualization concept
- Improve the ability of technology
- The business continuity also raised due to the use of virtualization
- It creates a mixed virtual environment
- Increase efficiency for development & test environment
- Loours Total Cost of Ownership (TCO)

3.3.3 Features of Virtualization

1. Partitioning: Multiple virtual servers can run on a physical server at the same time
2. Encapsulation of data: All data on the virtual server including boot disks is encapsulated in a file format
3. Isolation: The Virtual server running on the physical server are safely separated & don't affect each other
4. Hardware Independence: When the virtual server runs, it can migrate to the different hardware platform.

3.4 Types of Virtualization

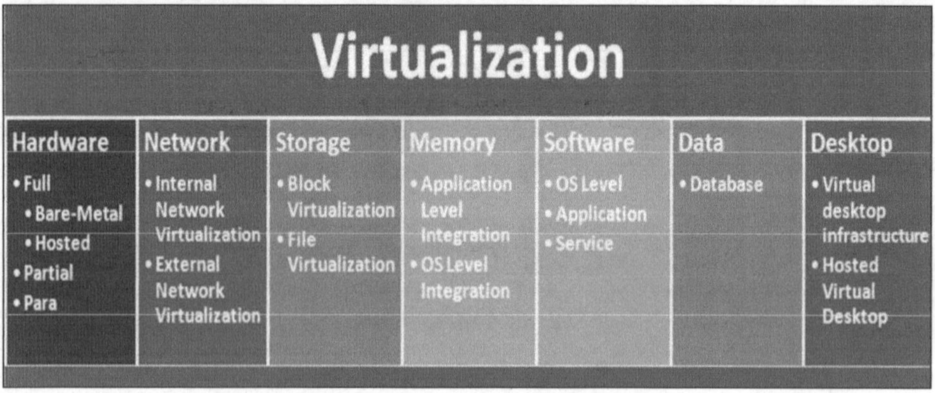

Fig. 3.6: Virtualization types

Seven types of Virtualization:

1. Hardware Virtualization.

2. Software Virtualization.
3. Network Virtualization.
4. Storage Virtualization
5. Memory Virtualization.
6. Data Virtualization.
7. Desktop Virtualization.

3.4.1 Hardware Virtualization

1. Hardware or platform virtualization means creation of virtual machine that act like realcomputer.
2. E.g. Computer running Microsoft Windows 7 may host the virtual machine look like a Ubundu.
3. Hardware virtualization also knows as hardware-assisted virtualization or server virtualization.
4. The basic idea of the technology is to combine many small physical servers into one largephysical server, so that the processor can be used more effectively and efficiently.
5. Each small server can host a virtual machine, but the entire cluster of servers is treated as asingle device by any process requesting the hardware.
6. The hardware resource allotment is done by the hypervisor.The advantages are
7. Increased processing poour as a result of maximized hardware utilization and **application uptime.**

Hardware virtualization is further subdivided into the following types.

1. **Full Virtualization:** Guest software does not require any modifications since the underlying hardwareis fully simulated.
2. **Para Virtualization:** The hardware is not simulated and the guest software run their own isolateddomains.
3. **Partial Virtualization:** The virtual machine simulates the hardware and becomes independent of it.The guest operating system may require modifications.

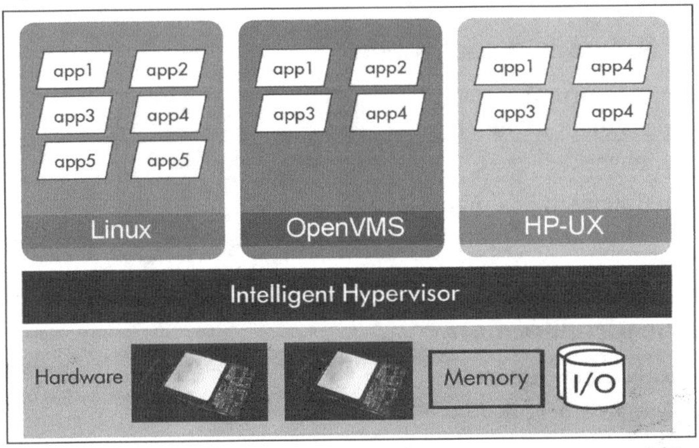

Fig. 3.7: Hardware Virtualization

3.4.2 Software Virtualization

1. The ability to computer to run and create **one or more virtual environments.**
2. It is used to enable a **computer system** in order to allow a guest OS to run.

   Ex. Linux to run as a guest that is natively running a Microsoft Windows OS.

Subtypes of Software Virtualization

- **Operating System Virtualization:** Hosting multiple OS on the native
- **Application Virtualization:** Hosting individual applications in a virtual environment separate from the native OS.
- **Service Virtualization:** Hosting specific processes and services related to a particularapplication

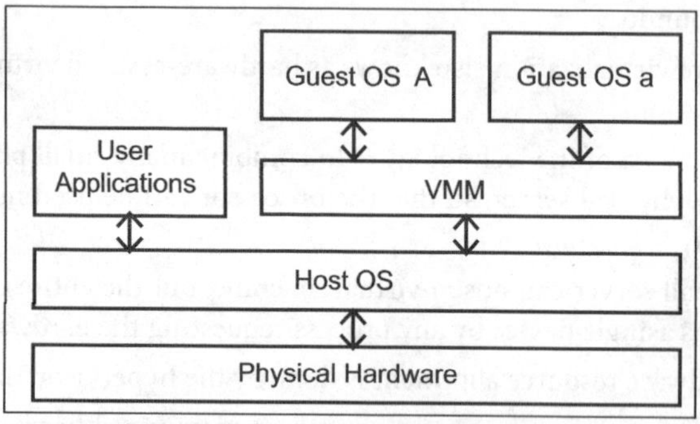

Fig. 3.8: Software Virtualization

3.4.3 Network Virtualization

1. It refers to the management and monitoring of a computer network as a single managerialentity from a single software-based administrator's console.
2. Multiple sub-networks can be created on the same physical network, which may or may notis authorized to communicate with each other.
3. It allows network optimization of data transfer rates, scalability, reliability, flexibility, and-security.

Subtypes of Network Virtualization

- **Internal network:** Enables a single system to function like a network
- **External network:** Combine many networks, or parts of networks into a virtual unit.

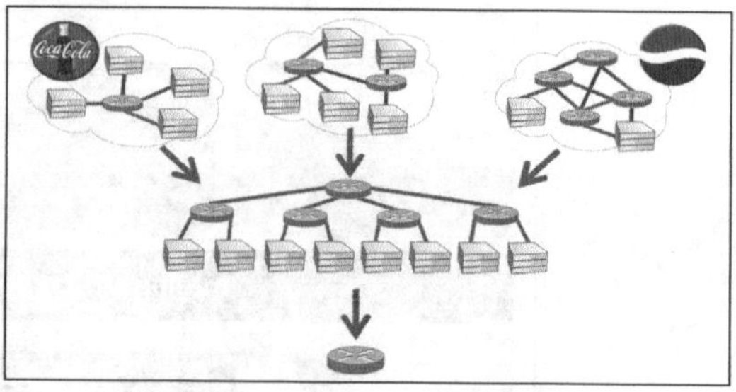

Fig. 3.9: Network Virtualization

3.4.4 Storage Virtualization

Multiple physical storage devices are grouped together, which look like a single storage device.

E.g. **Partitioning our hard drive** into multiple partitions

Advantages

a. Improved storage management in a heterogeneous IT environment
b. Easy updates, better availability
c. Reduced downtime
d. Better storage utilization
e. Automated management

Two types

- **Block**- Multiple storage devices are consolidated into one
- **File**- Storage system grants access to files that are stored over multiple hosts

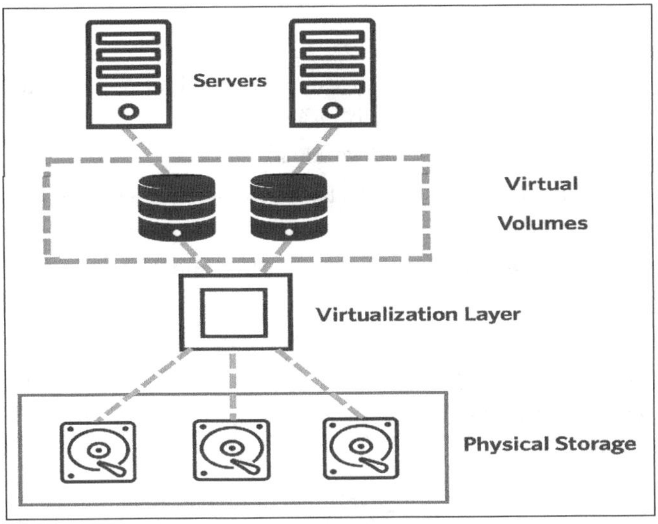

Fig. 3.10: Storage Virtualization

3.4.5 Memory Virtualization

1. The way to decouple memory from the server to provide a shared, distributed or networked function.
2. It enhances performance by providing greater memory capacity without any addition to the main memory.

Implementations

- **Application-level integration:** Applications access the memory pool directly

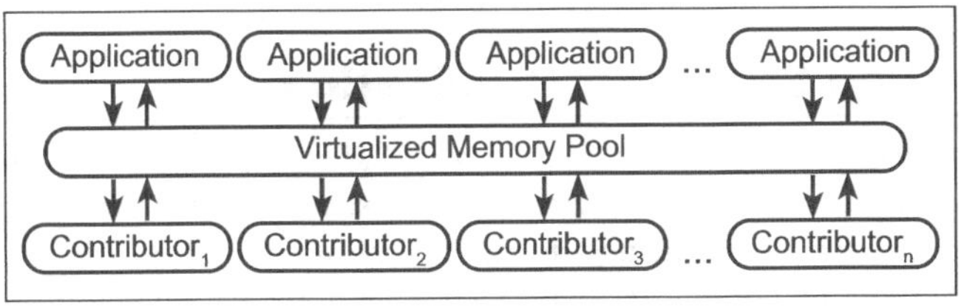

Fig. 3.11: Application level integration

- **Operating System Level Integration** – Access to the memory pool is provided through an operating system.

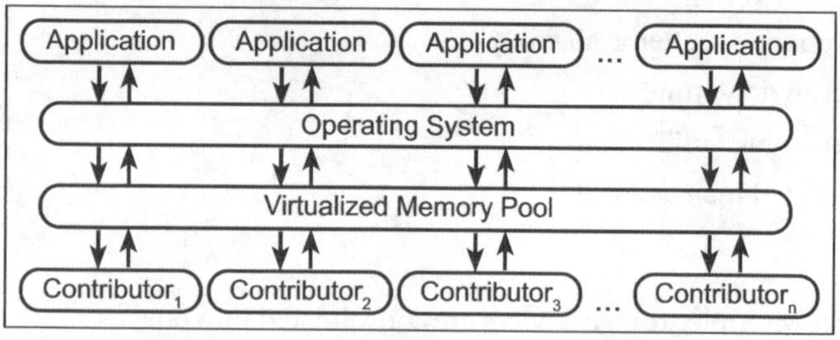

Fig. 3.12: Operating system level integration

3.4.6 Data Virtualization

1. Without any technical details, we can easily manipulate data and know how it is formatted orwhere it is physically located.
2. It decreases the data errors and workload.
3. The data is presented as an abstract layer completely independent of data structure anddatabase systems.
4. The user's desktop is stored on a remote server, allowing the user to access his/her desktopfrom any device or location.
5. It provides the work convenience and security.
6. It provides a lot of flexibility for employees to work from home or on the go.
7. Since the data transfer takes place over secure protocols, any risk of data theft is minimized.

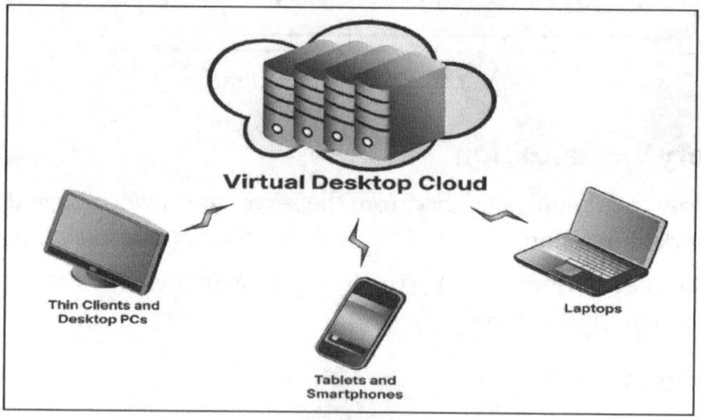

Fig. 3.13: Data virtualization

3.5 Operating System Virtualization

Operating system virtualization refers to the use of software to allow system hardware to run multiple instances of different operating systems concurrently, allowing we to run different applications requiring different operating systems on one computer system. The operating systems do not interfere with each other or the various applications. Not to be confused with operatingsystem-level virtualization, which is a type of server virtualization.

3.5.1 VMWare

VMware is a virtualization and cloud computing software provider based in Palo Alto, Calif. Foundedin 1998, VMware is a subsidiary of Dell Technologies. EMC Corporation originally acquired VMwarein 2004; EMC was later acquired by Dell Technologies in 2016. VMware bases its virtualization technologies on its bare-metal hypervisor ESX/ESXi in x86 architecture.With VMware server virtualization, a hypervisor is installed on the physical server to allow for multiple virtual machines (VMs) to run on the same physical server. Each VM can run its own operating system (OS),which means multiple OSes can run on one physical server. All the VMs on the same physical server share resources, such as networking and RAM. In 2019, VMware added support to its hypervisor to run containerized workloads in a Kubernetes cluster in a similar way. These types of workloads can bemanaged by the infrastructure team in the same way as virtual machines and the DevOps teams can deploy containers as they oure used to.

Diane Greene, Scott Devine, Mendel Rosenblum, Edward Wang and Edouard Bugnion founded VMware, which launched its first product -- VMware Workstation -- in 1999. The company released its second product, VMware ESX in 2001.VMware products include virtualization, networking and security management tools, software-defined data center software and storage software.VMware vSphere is VMware's suite of virtualization products. VMware vSphere, known as VMware Infrastructure prior to 2009, includes the following:

- ESXi
- vCenter Server
- vSphere Client
- vMotion

As of April 2018, the most current version is vSphere 6.7, which is available in three editions: Standard,Enterprise Plus and Platinum. There are also two three-server kits targeted toward small and medium- sized businesses named vSphere Essentials and Essentials Plus.With **VMware Cloud on AWS**, customers can run a cluster of vSphere hosts with vSAN and NSX in an Amazon data center and run their workloads there while in the meantime manage them with their well-known VMware tools and skills.

3.5.2 Networking and Security

VMware NSX is a virtual networking and security software offering created when VMware acquired Nicera in 2012. NSX allows an admin to virtualize network components, enabling them to develop, deploy and configure virtual networks and switches through software rather than hardware. A softwarelayer sits on top of the hypervisor to allow an administrator to divide a physical network into multiplevirtual networks.With the latest release of the product, NSX-T Data Center, network virtualization canbe added to both ESXi and KVM as hypervisors, as well as to bare-metal servers. Also containerized workloads in a Kubernetes cluster can be virtualized and protected. NSX-T Data Center also offers Network Function Virtualization, with which functions such as a firewall, load balancer and VPN, canbe run in the virtualization software stack.

VMware vRealize Network Insight is a network operations management tool that enables an admin to plan microsegmentation and check on the health of VMware NSX. VRealize Network Insight relieson technology from VMware's acquisition of Arkin in 2016. VRealize Network Insight collects information from the NSX Manager. It also displays errors in its user interface, which helps troubleshoot an NSX environment.

Software Defined Data Center (SDDC) Platform

VMware Cloud Foundation is an integrated software stack that bundles vSphere, VMware vSAN andVMware NSX into a single platform through the SDDC Manager. An admin can deploy the bundle onpremises as a private cloud or run it as a service within a public cloud. An administrator can provisionan application immediately without having to wait for network or storage.

Storage and Availability

- **VMware vSAN** is a software-based storage feature that is built into the ESXi hypervisor and integratedwith vSphere; it pools disk space from multiple ESXi hosts and provisions it via smart policies, such as protection limits, thin provisioning and erasure coding. It integrates with vSphere High Availabilityto offer increased compute and storage availability.
- **VMware Site Recovery Manager (SRM)** is a disaster recovery management product that allows an administrator to create recovery plans that are automatically executed in case of a failure. Site RecoveryManager allows admins to automatically orchestrate the failover and failback of VMs. SRM also integrates with NSX to preserve network and security policies on migrated VMs.
- **VMware vCloud NFV** is a network functions virtualization platform that enables a service provider to run network functions as virtualized applications from different vendors. NFV provides the same benefits of virtualization and cloud to a communications service provider that previously relied on hardware.

Cloud Management Platform

The **vRealize Suite** is a group of software that allows a user to create and manage hybrid clouds. The vRealize Suite includes vRealize Operations for monitoring, vRealize Log Insight for centralized logging, vRealize Automation for data center automation and vRealize Business for Cloud for cost management.

With this bundle, an administrator can deploy and manage VMs on multiple hypervisors or cloud platforms from a single management console. Released in 2019, VMware Tanzu allows customers to build containerized apps, run enterprise Kubernetes and manage Kubernetes for developers and IT.

Virtual Desktop Infrastructure

VMware Horizon allows organizations to run Windows desktops in the data center or in VMware Cloud on AWS. This removes the need to place and manage full desktops on the workplace and centralizes management and security for the user's environment. It integrates with the VMware productsApp Volumes and Dynamic Environment Manager for application delivery and Windows desktop management.

Digital Workspace and Enterprise Mobility Management

Workspace ONE allows an administrator to control mobile devices and cloud-hosted virtual desktops and applications from a single management platform deployed either in the cloud or on premises. TheWorkspace ONE suite includes VMware AirWatch, Horizon Air and Identity Manager. Identity Manager is an identity-as-a-service product that offers single sign-on (SSO) capabilities for web, cloudand mobile applications. Identity Manager gives SSO access to any application from any device, basedon the policies created. VMware AirWatch is an enterprise mobility management (EMM) software platform that enables an administrator to deploy and manage mobile devices, applications and data.

Personal Desktop

VMware Workstation is the first product ever released by the software company. It enables users to create and run VMs directly on a single Windows or Linux desktop or laptop. Those VMs run simultaneously with the physical machine. Each VM runs its own OS such as Windows or Linux.

This enables users to run Windows on a Linux machine or vice versa simultaneously with the natively installed OS. VMware Fusion is software like VMware Workstation that virtualizes a Windows or LinuxOS on Mac computers.

Benefits of VMware

1. Security based on a zero-trust model, along with better security than container systems like Kubernetes;
2. Better provisioning of applications and resources;
3. Simplified Data Center Management
4. Increased efficiency and agility of data center systems.

Drawbacks of VMware

1. High licensing fees;
2. Better Hyper-V and Xen hypervisor alternatives, according to some;
3. Lack of support and several bugs when used alongside oracle products; and
4. Hardware compatibility issues as not everything works well with VMware.

3.6 KVM

Kernel-based Virtual Machine (KVM) is an open source virtualization technology built into Linux®. Specifically, KVM lets we turn Linux into a hypervisor that allows a host machine to run multiple, isolated virtual environments called guests or virtual machines (VMs). KVM is part of Linux. If we've got Linux 2.6.20 or neour, we've got KVM. KVM was first announcedin 2006 and merged into the mainline Linux kernel version a year later. Because KVM is part of existingLinux code, it immediately benefits from every new Linux feature, fix, and advancement without additional engineering.

3.6.1 Working of KVM

KVM converts Linux into a type-1 (bare-metal) hypervisor. All hypervisors need some operating system-level components—such as a memory manager, process scheduler, input/output (I/O) ,stack, device drivers, security manager, a network stack, and more—to run VMs. KVM has all these components because it's part of the Linux kernel.

Every VM is implemented as a regular Linux process,scheduled by the standard Linux scheduler, with dedicated virtual hardware like a network card, graphics adapter, CPU(s), memory, and disks.

3.6.2 Implementing KVM

We need to have to run a version of Linux that was released after 2007 and it needs to be installed on X86 hardware that supports virtualization capabilities. If both of those boxes are checked, then all we have to do is load 2 existing modules (a host kernel module and a processor-specific module), an emulator, and any drivers that will help we run additional systems.

But implementing KVM on a supported Linux distribution—like Red Hat Enterprise Linux— expands KVM's capabilities, letting we swap resources among guests, share common libraries, optimize system performance, and a lot more.

3.6.3 Migrating to a KVM-based Virtual Infrastructure

Building a virtual infrastructure on a platform we're contractually tied to may limit our access to the source code. That means our IT developments are probably going to be more workarounds than innovations, and the next contract could keep we from investing in clouds, containers, and automation.Migrating to a KVM-based virtualization platform means being able to inspect, modify, and enhance the source code behind our hypervisor. And there's no enterprise-license agreement because there's no source code to protect.

3.6.4 KVM Features

KVM is part of Linux. Linux is part of KVM. Everything Linux has, KVM has too. But there arespecific features that make KVM an enterprise's preferred hypervisor.

Security

KVM uses a combination of security-enhanced Linux (SELinux) and secure virtualization (sVirt) for enhanced VM security and isolation. SELinux establishes security boundaries around VMs. sVirt extends SELinux's capabilities, allowing Mandatory Access Control (MAC) security to be applied to guest VMs and preventing manual labeling errors.

Storage

KVM is able to use any storage supported by Linux, including some local disks and network- attachedstorage (NAS). Multipath I/O may be used to improve storage and provide redundancy.

KVM also supports shared file systems so VM images may be shared by multiple hosts. Disk images support thin provisioning, allocating storage on demand rather than all up front.

Hardware Support

KVM can use a wide variety of certified Linux-supported hardware platforms. Because hardware vendors regularly contribute to kernel development, the latest hardware features are often rapidly adopted in the Linux kernel.

Memory Management

KVM inherits the memory management features of Linux, including non-uniform memory access andkernel same-page merging. The memory of a VM can be swapped, backed by large volumes for betterperformance, and shared or backed by a disk file.

Live Migration

KVM supports live migration, which is the ability to move a running VM between physical hosts withno service interruption. The VM remains powered on, network connections remain active, and applications continue to run while the VM is relocated. KVM also saves a VM's current state so it canbe stored and resumed later.

Performance and Scalability

KVM inherits the performance of Linux, scaling to match demand load if the number of guest machinesand requests increases. KVM allows the most demanding application workloads to be virtualized and is the basis for many enterprise virtualization setups, such as datacenters and private clouds

Scheduling and Resource Control

In the KVM model, a VM is a linux process, scheduled and managed by the kernel. The Linux scheduler allows fine-grained control of the resources allocated to a Linux process and guarantees a quality of service for a particular process. In KVM, this includes the completely fair scheduler, control groups, network name spaces, and real-time extensions.

Lower Latency and Higher Prioritization

The Linux kernel features real-time extensions that allow VM-based apps to run at lower latency.The kernel also divides processes that require long computing times into smaller components, which are then scheduled and processed accordingly.

Managing KVM

It's possible to manually manage a handful of VM fired up on a single workstation without a management tool. Large enterprises use virtualization management software that interfaces with virtual environments and the underlying physical hardware to simplify resource administration, enhance data analyses, and streamline operations. Red Hat created Red Hat Virtualization for exactly this purpose.

KVM and Red Hat

We believe in KVM so much that it's the sole hypervisor for all of our virtualization products, and we're continually improving the kernel code with contributions to the KVM community. But since

KVM is part of Linux, it's already included in Red Hat Enterprise Linux. Red Hat has 2 versions of KVM. The KVM that ships with Red Hat Enterprise Linux has all of the hypervisor functionality with basic management capabilities, allowing customers to run up to 4 isolated virtual machines on a single host. Red Hat Virtualization contains an advanced version of KVM that enables enterprise management of unlimited guest machines. It's ideal for use in datacenter virtualization, technical workstations, private clouds, and in development or production.

3.7 System VM and Process VM

Two Categories of Virtual Machines

Virtual machines are separated in two major categories, based on their use and degree of correspondence to any real machine. A system virtual machine provides a complete system platform which supports the execution of a complete operating system (OS). In contrast, a process virtual machine is designed to run a single program, which means that it supports a single process. An essential characteristic of a virtual machine is that the software running inside is limited to the resources and abstractions provided by the virtual machine — it cannot break out of its virtual world.

3.7.1 System Virtual Machines

System virtual machines (sometimes called hardware virtual machines) allow the sharing of the underlying physical machine resources between different virtual machines, each running its own operating system.

The software layer providing the virtualization is called a virtual machine monitor or hypervisor. A hypervisor can run on bare hardware (Type 1 or native VM) or on top of an operating system (Type 2 or hosted VM).

Main Advantages of System VMs

- Multiple OS environments can co-exist on the same computer, in strong isolation from eachother;
- The virtual machine can provide an instruction set architecture (ISA) that is somewhat differentfrom that of the real machine.

Main Disadvantages of System VMs

- There's still an overhead of the virtualization solution which is used to run and manage a VM, soperformance of a VM will be somewhat slower compared to a physical system with comparableconfiguration
- Virtualization means decoupling from physical hardware available to the host PC, this usually means access to devices needs to go through the virtualization solution and this may not alwaysbe possible

Multiple VMs each running their own operating system (called guest operating system) are frequentlyused in server consolidation, where different services that used to run on individual machines in orderto avoid interference are instead run in separate VMs on the same physical machine. This use is frequently called quality-of-service isolation (QoS isolation).

3.7.2 Process Virtual Machines

A process VM, sometimes called an application virtual machine, runs as a normal application inside anOS and supports a single process. It is created when that process is started and destroyed when it exits. Its purpose is to provide a platform-independent programming environment that abstracts away detailsof the underlying hardware or operating system, and allows a program to execute in the same way on any platform.

A process VM provides a high-level abstraction — that of a high-level programming language (compared to the low-level ISA abstraction of the system VM). Process VMs are implemented using an interpreter; performance comparable to compiled programming languages is achieved by the use ofjust-in-time compilation. This type of VM has become popular with the Java programming language, which is implemented using the Java virtual machine. Another example is the.NET Framework, whichruns on a VM called the Common Language Runtime.

3.8 Virtual Machine Monitor

A Virtual Machine Monitor (VMM) is a software program that enables the creation, management and governance of virtual machines (VM) and manages the operation of a virtualized environment on top of a physical host machine. VMM is also known as Virtual Machine Manager and Hypervisor. VMM is the primary software behind virtualization environments and implementations. When installed over a host machine, VMM facilitates the creation of VMs, each with separate operating systems (OS)and applications. VMM manages the backend operation of these VMs by allocating the necessary computing, memory, storage and other input/output (I/O) resources. VMM also provides a centralized interface for managing the entire operation, status and availability ofVMs that are installed over a single host or spread across different and interconnected hosts.

The software that creates a virtual machine (VM) environment in a computer In a regular, non- virtual computer, the operating system is the master control program, which manages the execution of all applications and acts as an interface between the apps and the hardware. The OS has the highest privilege level in the machine, known as "ring 0"

In a VM environment, the VM monitor (VMM) becomes the master control program with the highest privilege level, and the VMM manages one or more "guest operating systems." Each guest OS manages its own applications in a separate "virtual machine" (VM) in the computer, sometimes called a "guest OS stack."

The VM monitor (VMM) is an interface between the guest OS and the hardware. It intercepts calls to the peripheral devices and memory tables from each guest OS and intercedes on its behalf.

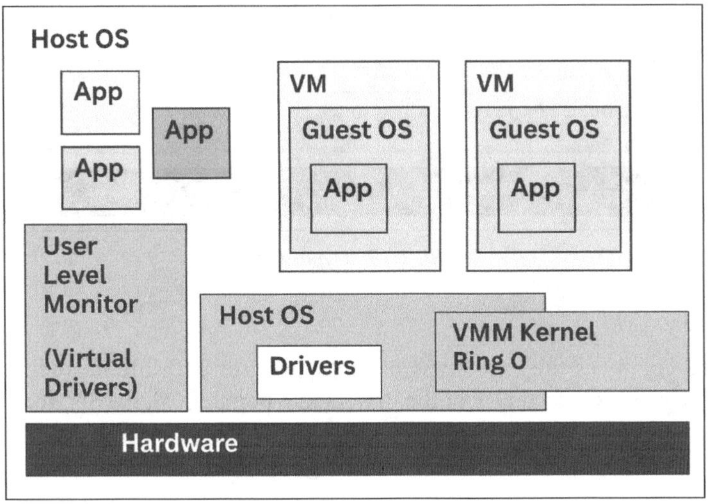

Fig. 3.14: Host OS monitor

Host OS

This VM monitor (VMM) is installed in an existing, running computer. The VMM kernel runs alongside the host OS, and calls for I/O are redirected to virtual drivers that call the native API of the host OS. Examples of OS-hosted VMMs are VMware Workstation, VMware Server, Parallels Workstation and Parallels Desktop for Mac.

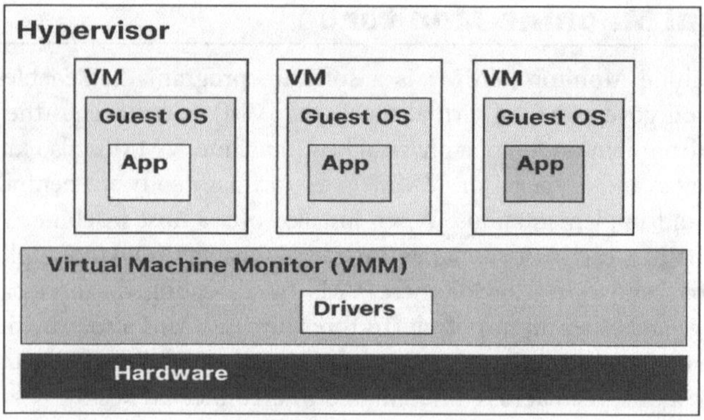

Fig. 3.15: VM monitor

Hypervisor

The hypervisor monitor provides the most control, flexibility and performance, because it is not subjectto limitations of a host OS. The hypervisor relies on its own software drivers for the hardware; however,they may limit portability to another platform. Examples of this method are VMware ESX and IBM's mainframe z/VM.

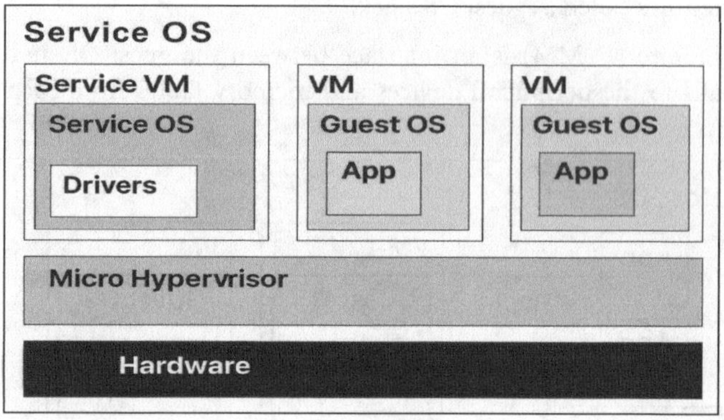

Fig. 3.16: Hypervisor

Service OS

This method combines the robustness of the hypervisor with the flexibility of the host model. In orderto take advantage of the drivers in a popular OS, the Service OS runs as a component of the hypervisorin a separate VM. Xen, XenServer and Hyper-V are examples of the service VM approach. The VMMis in charge of running the virtual machines.

There are two Main Types of VMM:

- **Type 1**: Native Hypervisors run directly on the host machine, and share out resources (such as memoryand devices) between guest machines.

  e.g. XEN, Oracle VM Server

- **Type 2:** Hosted Hypervisors run as an application inside an operating system, and support virtualmachines running as individual processes.

  e.g. VirtualBox, Parallels Desktop, QEMU

Properties of a Virtual Machine

1. **Efficiency:** The majority of guest instructions are executed directly on the host machine.
2. **Resource Control:** The virtual machine monitor must remain in control of all machine resources.
3. **Equivalence:** The virtual machine must behave in a way that is indistinguishable from if it wasrunning as a physical machine.

Efficiency

"All innocuous instructions are executed by the hardware directly, with no intervention at all on thepart of the control program."

Normal guest machine instructions should be executed directly on the processor. System instructionsneed to be emulated by the VMM.

Resource Control

"It must be impossible for that arbitrary program to affect the system resources, i.e. memory, availableto it; the allocator of the control program is to be invoked upon any attempt." The virtual machine should not be able to affect the host machine in any adverse way. The host machine should remain in control of all physical resources, sharing them out to guest machines.

Equivalence

"Any program K executing with a control program resident, with two possible exceptions, performs ina manner indistinguishable from the case when the control program did not exist and K had whatever freedom of access to privileged instructions that the programmer had intended." A formal way of sayingthat the operating system running on a virtual machine should believe it is running on a physical machine, i.e. the behaviour of the virtual machine (from the guest OS' point of view) is identical to thatof the corresponding physical machine. The two exceptions mentioned are: temporal latency (some instruction sequences will take longer torun) and resource availability (physical machine resources are shared between virtual machines).

High Level Language Virtual Machines (HLL VM)

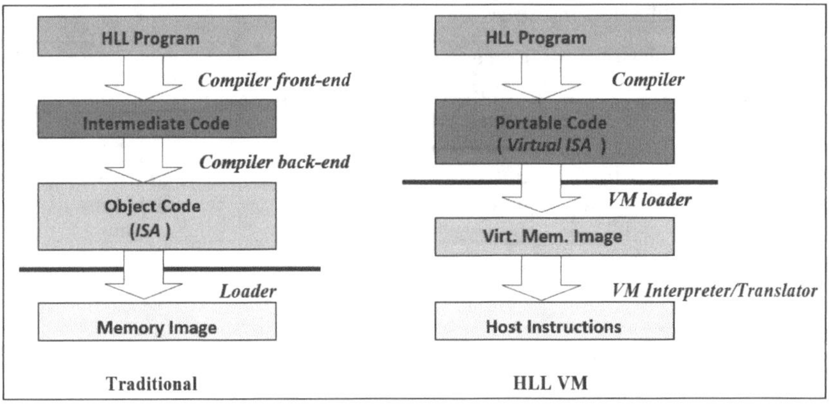

Fig. 3.17: Traditional vs HLL VM

Two major examples: Java VM

Microsoft Common Language Infrastructure (CLI)

HLL VMs

1. Compiler forms program files (e.g. class files)
2. Program files contain both code and metadata.

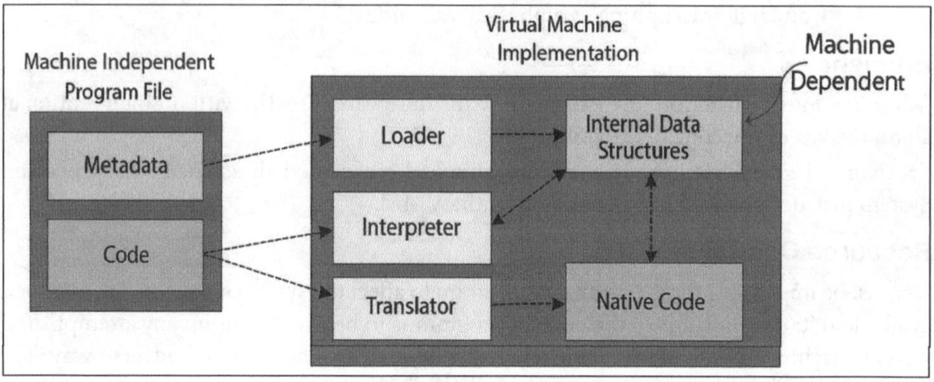

Fig. 3.18: Traditional vs HLL VM

Characteristics of HLL VMs

1. Security
2. Robustness
3. Networking
4. Performance

1. Security

1. A key aspect of modern network-oriented VMs
2. Must protect:
   a. Local files and resources
   b. Runtime from user process
3. The program runs in a sandbox at the host machine. It is managed by the VM runtime.
4. The ability to load an untrusted application and run it in a managed secure fashion is a very big challenge!

2. Robustness: Object Orientation

i. Objects

- Data carrying entities
- Dynamically allocated
- Must be accessed via pointers or references

ii. Methods

- Procedures that operate on objects

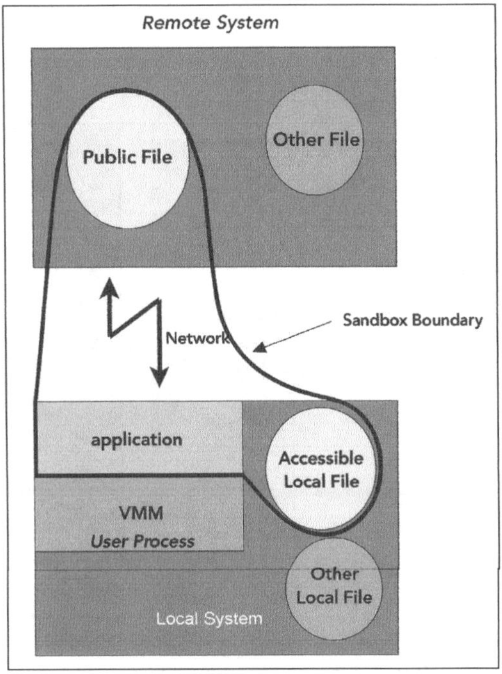

Fig. 3.19: *HLL VM*

iii. Class

1. A type of object and its associated methods
2. Object created at runtime is an instance of the class
3. Data associated with a class may be dynamic or static

OO programming paradigm has become the model of choice for modern HLL VMs. Both Java and CLI are designed to support OO software.

3. Networking

The application must use the available bandwidth (scarce) efficiently

1. Application loaded incrementally dynamic linking
2. Improves program startup-time

JVM: Bytcode Emulation

a. Interpretation
b. Simple, fast startup, but slow
c. Compile each method when first touched
d. Simple, static optimizations
e. Hot-Spot Compilation
f. JFind frequently executed code

g. Apply more aggressive optimizations on that code.
h. Typically phased with interpretation or JIT
i. Dynamic Compilation
j. Based on Hot-Spot compilation
k. Use runtime information to optimize

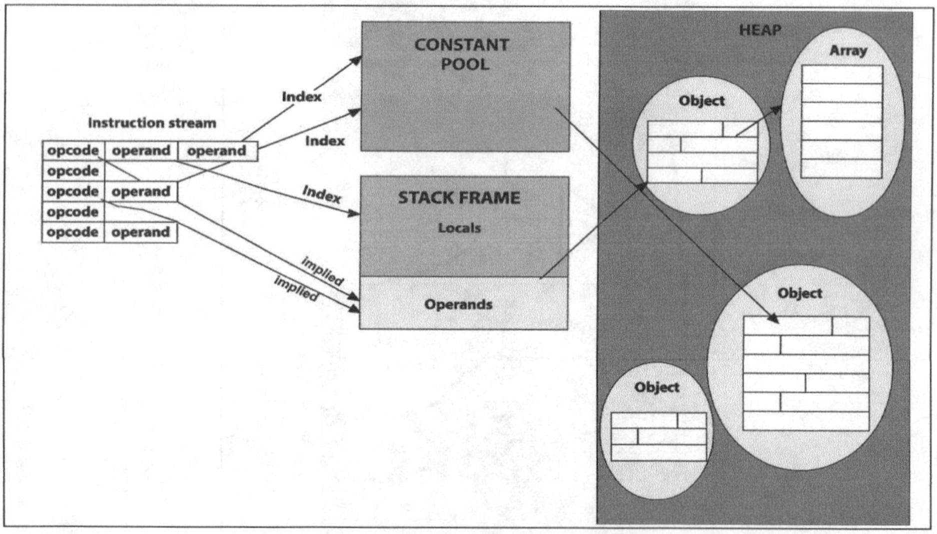

Fig. 3.20: Memory Hierarchy in JVM

3.9 Hypervisor

Software that controls the layer between the hardware operating systems. It allows multiple operating systems to run on the same physical hardware. There are two types of hypervisors:

- Bare metal, which allows the hypervisor to run directly on the hardware
- Hosted architecture, in which the hypervisor runs on top of an existing operating system

A low-level program is required to provide system resource access to virtual machines, and this program is referred to as the hypervisor or Virtual Machine Monitor (VMM). A hypervisor running on bare metal is a Type 1 VM or native VM. Examples of Type 1 Virtual Machine Monitors are LynxSecure, RTS Hypervisor, Oracle VM, Sun xVM Server, VirtualLogix VLX, VMware ESX and ESXi, and Wind River VxWorks, among others. The operating system loade dinto a virtual machine is referred to as the guest operating system, and there is no constraint on running the same guest on multiple VMs on a physical system. Type 1 VMs have no host operating system because they are installed on a bare system.

An operating system running on a Type 1 VM is a full virtualization because it is a complete simulation of the hardware that it is running on. Not all CPUs support virtual machines, and many that do require that we enable this support in the BIOS. For example, AMD-V processors(code named Pacifica) and Intel VT-x (code named Vanderpool) oure the first of these vendor's64-bit offerings that added this type of support.

Some hypervisors are installed over an operating system and are referred to as Type 2 or hosted VM. Examples of Type 2 Virtual Machine Monitors are Containers, KVM, Microsoft Hyper V,Parallels Desktop for Mac, Wind River Simics, VMWare Fusion, Virtual Server 2005 R2, Xen,Windows Virtual PC, and VMware Workstation 6.0 and Server, among others. This is a very rich product category. Type 2 virtual machines are installed over a host operating system; for Microsoft Hyper-V, that operating system would be Windows Server. In the section that follows,the Xen hypervisor (which runs on top of a Linux host OS) is more fully described. Xen is usedby Amazon Web Services to provide Amazon Machine Instances (AMIs). On a Type 2 VM, a software interface is created that emulates the devices with which a system would normally interact. This abstraction is meant to place many I/O operations outside the virtual environment, which makes it both pro grammatically easier and more efficient to execute device I/O than it would be inside a virtual environment. This type of virtualization is sometimes referred to as para-virtualization, and it is found in hypervisors such as Microsoft's Hyper-V andXen. It is the host operating system that is performing the I/O through a para-API.

3.9.1 VMware's vSphere Cloud Computing Infrastructure Model

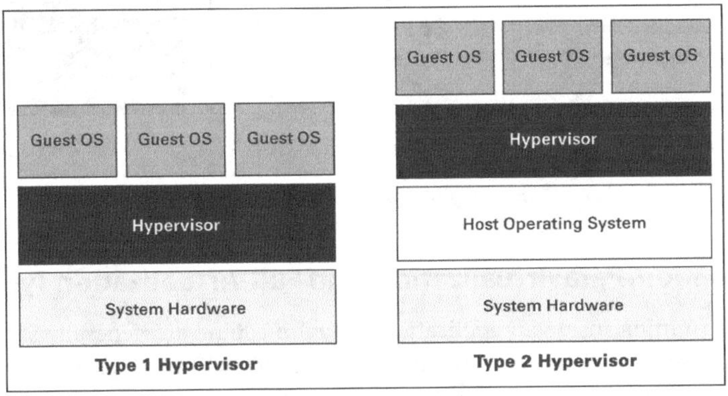

Fig. 3.21: Hypervisor

3.9.2 Type 1 and Type 2 Hypervisors

The above figure shows the difference between emulation, para virtualization, and full virtualization. In emulation, the virtual machine simulates hardware, so it can be independent of the underlying system hardware. A guest operating system using emulation does not needto be modified in any way. Para virtualization requires that the host operating system provide a virtual machine interface for the guest operating system and that the guest access hardwarethrough that host VM. An operating system running as a guest on a paravirtualizationsystemmust be ported to work with the host interface.

Finally, in a full virtualization scheme, the VM is installed as a Type 1 Hypervisor directly onto the hardware. All operating systems infull virtualization communicate directly with the VM hypervisor, so guest operating systemsdo not require any modification. Guest operating systems in full virtualization systems are generally faster than other virtualization schemes. The Virtual Machine Interface (VMI) open standard (http://vmi ncsa.uiuc.edu/) that VMware has proposed is an example of a paravirtualization API. The latest version of VMI is 2.1, andit ships as a default installation with many versions of the Linux operating system. Wikipedia maintains a page called "Comparison of platform virtual machines" http://en.wikipedia.org/wiki/Comparison of platform virtual machines. The page contains a table of features of the most common Virtual Machine Managers. Mostly all are familiar with process or application virtual machines.

Most folks run the Java Virtual Machine or Microsoft's.NET Framework VM (called the Common Language Runtime or CLR) on their computers. A process virtual machine instantiates when a command begins a process, the VM is created by an interpreter, the VM then executes the process, and finally the VM exits the system and is destroyed. During the time the VM exists,it runs as a high-level abstraction.

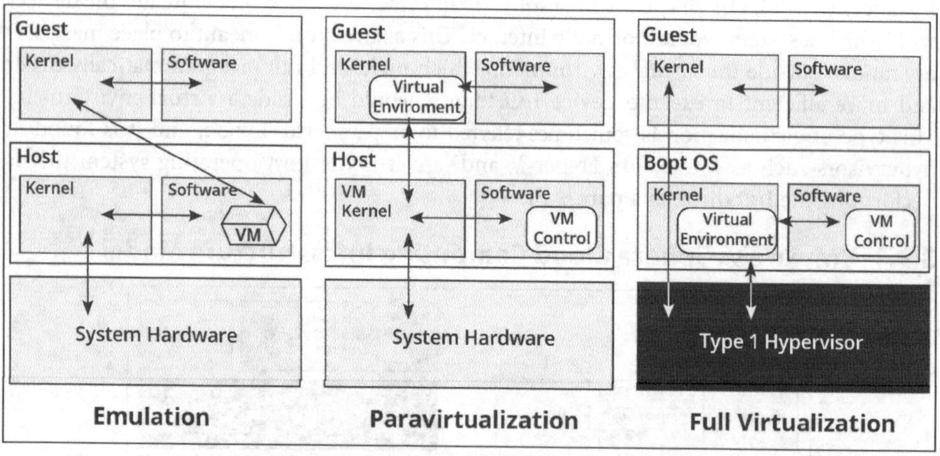

Fig. 3.22: Types of virtualization

3.9.3 Emulation, Paravirtualization, and Full Virtualization Types

Applications running inside an application virtual machine are generally slow, but these programs are very popular because they provide portability, offer rich programming languages,come with many advanced features, and allow platform independence for their programs. Although many cloud computing applications provide process virtual machine applications, this type of abstraction isn't really suitable for building a large or high-performing cloud network, with one exception. The exception is the process VMs that enable a class of parallel cluster computing applications. These applications are high- performance systems where the virtual machine is operating one process per cluster node, and the system maintains the necessary intra-application communications over the network interconnect. Examples of this type of system are the Parallel Virtual Machine (PVM; see http://www.csm.ornl.gov/pvm/pvm home.html) and the Message Passing Interface (MPI; see http://www mpi-forum.org/).

Some people do not consider these application VMs to be true virtual machines, noting that these applications can still access the host operating system services on the specific system on which they are running. The emphasis on using these process VMs is in creating a high- performance networked supercomputer often out of heterogeneous systems, rather than on creating a ubiquitous utility resource that characterizes a cloud network.

Some operating systems such as Sun Solaris and IBM AIX 6.1 support a feature known as operating system virtualization. This type of virtualization creates virtual servers at the operating system or kernel level. Each virtual server is running in its own virtual environment (VE) as a virtual private server (VPS). Different operating systems use different names to describe these machine instances, each of which can support its own guest OS. However, unlike true virtual machines, VPS must all be running the same OS and the same version of that OS. Sun Solaris 10uses VPS to create what is called Solaris Zones. With IBM AIX, the VPS is called a System Workload Partition (WPAR). This type of virtualization allows for a dense collection of virtual machines with relatively low overhead. Operating system virtualization provides many of the benefits of virtualization previously noted in this section.

3.10 Xen Hypervisor

Xen Hypervisor Xen is a type-1 hypervisor, providing services that allow multiple computer operating systems to execute on the same computer hardware concurrently. It was developed bythe University of Cambridge. Now being developed by the Linux Foundation with support fromIntel.

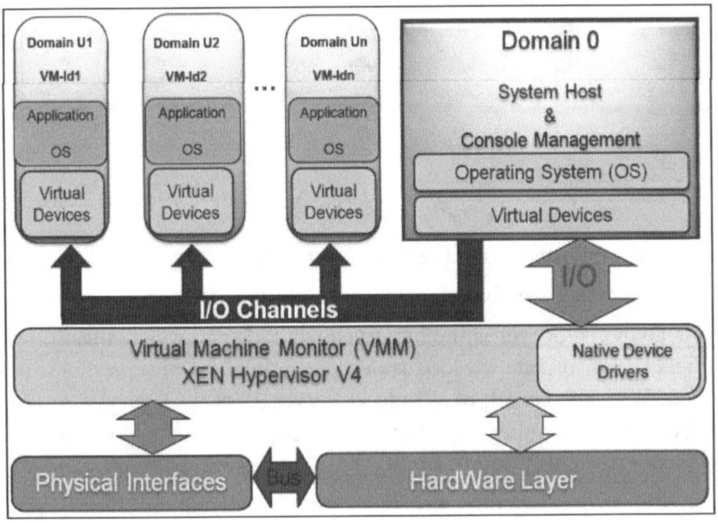

Fig. 3.23: Xen

Xen is a hypervisor that enables the simultaneous creation, execution and management of multiplevirtual machines on one physical computer.

- Xen was developed by XenSource, which was purchased by Citrix Systems in 2007.
- Xen was first released in 2003.
- It is an open source hypervisor.
- It also comes in an enterprise version.
- Because it's a type-1 hypervisor, Xen controls, monitors and manages the hardware,peripheral and I/O resources directly.
- Guest virtual machines request Xen to provision any resource and must install Xenvirtual device drivers to access hardware components.
- Xen supports multiple instances of the same or different operating systems with nativesupport for most operating systems, including Windows and Linux.
- Moreover, Xen can be used on x86, IA-32 and ARM processor architecture.

3.11 Hyper V

Microsoft **Hyper-V**, formerly known as **Windows Server Virtualization**, is a native hypervisor; it can create virtual machines on x86-64 systems running Windows. Starting with Windows 8, Hyper-V supersedes Windows Virtual PC as the hardware virtualization component of the client editions of Windows NT. A server computer running Hyper-V can be configured to expose individual virtual machines to one or more networks.

Hyper-V was first released alongside Windows Server 2008, and has been available without charge for all the Windows Server and some client operating systems since.

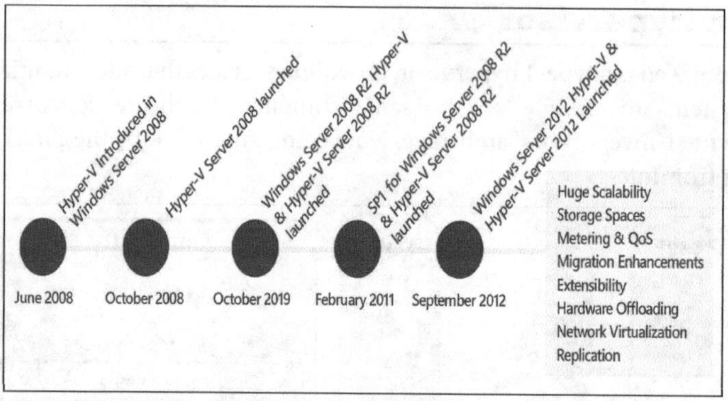

Fig. 3.24: Hyper V

There are two manifestations of the Hyper-V technology:

Hyper-V is the hypervisor-based virtualization role of **Windows Server**.

Microsoft Hyper-V Server is the hypervisor-based server virtualization product that allowscustomers to consolidate workloads onto a single physical server. This is available as a freedownload. With the launch of Windows Server 2008 R2 Hyper-V, in October 2009, Microsoft introduced a number of compelling capabilities to help organizations reduce costs, whilst increasing agility and flexibility. Key features introduced included:

- **Live Migration:** Enabling the movement of virtual machines (VMs) with no interruption or downtime
- **Cluster Shared Volumes:** Highly scalable and flexible use of shared storage (SAN) for VMs
- **Processor Compatibility:** Increase the Flexibility for Live Migration across hosts with differing CPU architectures
- **Hot Add Storage:** Flexibly add or remove storage to and from VMs
- **Improved Virtual Networking Performance:** Support for Jumbo Frames and Virtual Machine Queue (VMq)

With the addition of Service Pack 1 (SP1) for Hyper-V, in October 2011, Microsoft introduced 2 new, key capabilities to help organizations realize even greater value from the platform:

- **Dynamic Memory:** More efficient use of memory while maintaining consistent workload performance and scalability.
- **RemoteFX**: Provides the richest virtualized Windows 7 experience for Virtual Desktop Infrastructure (VDI) deployments.

3.11.1 Windows Server 2012 Hyper V and Windows Server 2012 R2

Fast forward to September 2012, and the launch of Windows Server 2012. This brought an incredible number of new and an enhanced Hyper-V capabilities. These capabilities, many of which we'll discuss in this paper, ranged from enhancements around scalability, new storage and networking features, significant enhancements to the Live Migration capabilities,deeper integration with hardware, and an in-box VM replication capability, to name but a few.

These improvements, new features and enhancements can be grouped into 4 key areas,and it's these key areas we'll focus on throughout this whitepaper, looking at both Windows Server 2012 and R2, and how it compares and contrasts with vSphere 5.5. The 4 key areas are:

- **Scalability, Performance & Density:** customers are looking to run bigger, more poourful virtual machines, to handle the demands of their biggest workloads. In addition, as hardwarescale grows, customers wish to take advantage of the largest physical systems to drive the highest levels of density, and reduce overall costs.
- **Security &Multitenancy**- Virtualized data centers are becoming more popular and practical every day. IT organizations and hosting providers have begun offering infrastructure as a service (IaaS), which provides more flexible, virtualized infrastructures to customers— "server instances on-demand." Because of this trend, IT organizations and hosting providersmust offer customers enhanced security and isolation from one another, and in some cases, encrypted to meet compliance demands.
- **Flexible Infrastructure:** In a modern datacenter, customers are looking to be agile, in orderto respond to changing business demands quickly, and efficiently. Being able to move workloads flexibly around the infrastructure is of incredible importance, and in addition, customers want to be able to choose where best to deploy their workloads based on the needsof that workload specifically.
- **High Availability & Resiliency:** As customers' confidence in virtualization grows, and they virtualize their more mission-critical workloads, the importance of keeping those workloads continuously available grows significantly. Having capabilities built into the platform that not only help keep those workloads highly available, but also, in the event ofadisaster, quick to restore in another geographical location, is of immense importance when choosing a platform for today's modern datacenter.

3.11.2 Need for Hyper-V

Virtualization technologies help customers' loour costs and deliver greater agility and economies of scale. Either as a stand-alone product or an integrated part of Windows Server, Hyper-V is a leading virtualization platform for today and the transformational opportunity with cloud computing. With Hyper-V, it is now easier than ever for organizations to take advantage of the cost savings of virtualization, and make the optimum use of server hardware investments by consolidating multiple server roles as separate virtual machines that are running on a single physical machine. Customers can use Hyper-V to efficiently run multiple operating systems,Windows, Linux, and others, in parallel, on a single server. Windows Server 2012 R2 extendsthis with more features, greater scalability and further inbuilt reliability mechanisms. In the data center, on the desktop, and now in the cloud, the Microsoft virtualization platform, which is led by Hyper-V and surrounding System Center management tools, simply makes more sense and offers better value for money when compared to the competition.

Enhanced Storage Capabilities

Windows Server 2012 and subsequently, 2012 R2 Hyper-V also introduce a number of enhanced storage capabilities to support the most intensive, mission-critical of workloads. These capabilities include:

Virtual Fiber Channel: Enables virtual machines to integrate directly into Fiber Channel Storage Area Networks (SAN), unlocking scenarios such as fiber channel- based Hyper-V Guest Clusters.

	Resource	Windows Server 2008 R2 Hyper-V	Windows Server 2012 R2 Hyper-V	Improvement Factor
Host	Logical Processors	64	320	5×
	Physical Memory	1TB	4TB	4×
	Virtual CPUs per Host	512	2,048	4×
VM	Virtual CPUs per VM	4	64	16×
	Memroy per VM	64GB	1TB	16×
	Active VMs per Host	384	1,024	2.7×
	Guest NUMA	No	Yes	,
Cluster	Maximum Nodes	16	64	4×
	Maximum VMs	1,000	8,000	8×

Fig. 3.25: Hyper V comparision

- **Support for 4-KB Disk Sectors in Hyper-V Virtual Disks:** Support for 4,000-byte (4-KB) disk sectors lets customers take advantage of the emerging innovation in storage hardware that provides increased capacity and reliability.
- **New in R2 - Storage Spaces with Tiering:** Storage Spaces enables we to virtualize storageby grouping industry-standard disks into storage pools, and then create virtual disks called storage spaces from the available capacity in the storage pools. These pools now support a mix of HDD and SSD, providing a tiered pool, where hot data will reside on SSD and cold data on HDD. Fully supported as a repository for Hyper- V VMs.
- **Data Deduplication:** Windows Server 2012 R2 also provides an inbox deduplication capabilities which utilizes sub-file variable-size chunking and compression to considerably reduce storage consumption for files and folders hosted on deduplicated Windows Server volumes. With Windows Server 2012 R2, support has been added for VDI deployments. Deduplication rates for VDI deployments can range as high as 95% savings and that includesVDI deployments that utilize differencing disks for rapid provisioning.

- **New Virtual Hard Disk Format:** This new format, called VHDX, is designed to better handle current and future workloads and addresses the technological demands of an enterprise's evolving needs by increasing storage capacity, protecting data, improving quality performance on 4-KB disks, and providing additional operation- enhancing features.The maximum size of a VHDX file is 64TB.
- **Offloaded Data Transfer (ODX):** With Offloaded Data Transfer support, the Hyper- V hostCPUs can concentrate on the processing needs of the application and offload storage-relatedtasks to the SAN, increasing performance.
- **Online Checkpoint Merge**: With the online checkpoint merge capability, customers who have taken checkpoints (snapshots), for a running virtual machine, no longer have to poour down the virtual machine in order to merge the checkpoint back into the original virtual disk file, ensuring virtual machine uptime is increased and the administrator gains increased flexibility.
- **New in R2 – Online Virtual Disk Resize**: With the online virtual disk resize, administratorscan grow and shrink virtual disks that are attached to a VM's virtual SCSI controller, providing an administrator with greater flexibility to respond to changing business needs.

Enhanced Networking Performance

Windows Server 2012 R2 Hyper-V also includes a number of performance enhancements within the networking stack to help customers virtualize their most intensive network workloads. These capabilities include:

- **Dynamic Virtual Machine Queue:** DVMQ dynamically distributes incoming VM networktraffic processing to host processors (based on processor usage and network load). In times of heavy network load, Dynamic VMQ automatically recruits more processors. In times of light network load, Dynamic VMQ relinquishes those same processors
- **IPsec Task Offload:** IPsec Task Offload in Windows Server 2012 R2 leverages the hardware capabilities of server NICs to offload IPsec processing. This reduces the CPU overhead of IPsec encryption and decryption significantly. In Windows Server 2012 R2, IPsec Task Offload is extended to Virtual Machines as well. Customers using VMs who wantto protect their network traffic with IPsec can take advantage of the IPsec hardware offload capability available in server NICs, thus freeing up CPU cycles to perform more application level work and leaving the per packet encryption/decryption to hardware.
- **SR-IOV:** When it comes to virtual networking, a primary goal is native I/O throughput. Windows Server 2012 R2 provides the ability to assign SR-IOV functionality from physicaldevices directly into virtual machines. This gives VMs the ability to bypass the software- based Hyper-V Virtual Network Switch, and more directly address the NIC. As a result, CPUoverhead and latency is reduced, with a corresponding rise in throughput. This is all available, without sacrificing key Hyper- V features such as virtual machine Live Migration.
- **New in R2 – Virtual Receive Side Scaling:** Prior to 10GbE networking, one modern processor was usually more than enough to handle the networking workload of

a VM. Withthe introduction of 10GbE NICs, the amount of data being sent to and received from a VM exceeded what a single processor could effectively handle. In the physical host, this challengehad a solution, namely, Receive Side Scaling (RSS). RSS spreads traffic from the network interface card (NIC), based on TCP flows, and to multiple processors for simultaneous processing of TCP flows. With Windows Server 2012 R2 however, similar to how RSS distributes networking traffic to multiple cores in physical machines, vRSS spreads networking traffic to multiple VPs in each VM by enabling RSS inside the VM. With vRSSenabled, a VM is able to process traffic on multiple VPs simultaneously and increase the amount of throughput it is able to handle.

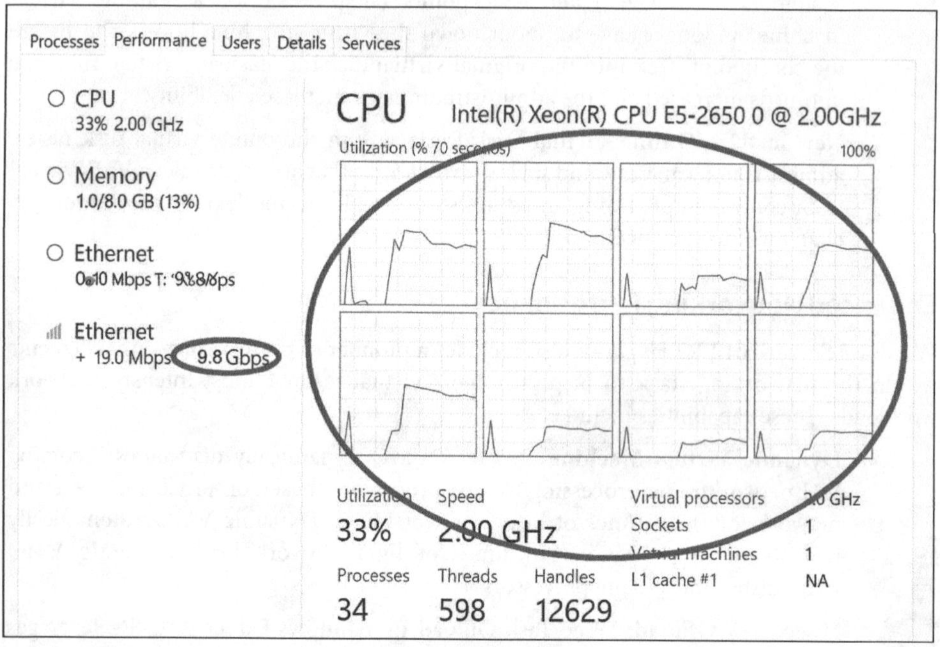

Fig. 3.26: CPU utilization

Enhanced Resource Management

Windows Server 2012 R2 Hyper-V also includes a number of enhanced resource management capabilities that help customers to optimize the utilization of the virtualized infrastructure to drive higher levels of performance. These capabilities include:

- **Dynamic Memory Improvements:** These improvements dramatically increase virtual machine consolidation ratios and improve reliability for restart operations that can lead to loour costs, especially in environments, such as VDI, that have many idle or low-load virtual machines. Administrators can now more flexibly manage memory through the use of aStartup, Minimum and Maximum configuration option, along with the ability to adjust the memory values whilst the VM is running, increasing flexibility for the administrator.

  Windows Server 2012 R2 Hyper-V also includes a capability known as Smart Paging, whichprovides a more reliable and robust solution for VM restarts when memory is undercontention.

- **Resource Metering:** In Windows Server 2012 R2 Hyper-V, Resource Metering, helps we track historical data on the use of virtual machines and gain insight into the resource use of specific servers. We can use this data to perform capacity planning, to monitor consumptionby different business units or customers, or to capture data needed to help redistribute the costs of running a workload. Resource Metering captures metrics across CPU, Memory, Diskand Network.
- **Network Quality of Service:** QoS provides the ability to programmatically adhere to a service level agreement (SLA) by specifying the minimum bandwidth that is available to a virtual machine or a port. It prevents latency issues by allocating maximum bandwidth use for a virtual machine or port.
- **New in R2: Storage Quality of Service:** Storage QoS provides storage performance isolation in a multitenant environment and mechanisms to notify we when the storage I/O performance does not meet the defined threshold to efficiently run our virtual machine workloads.

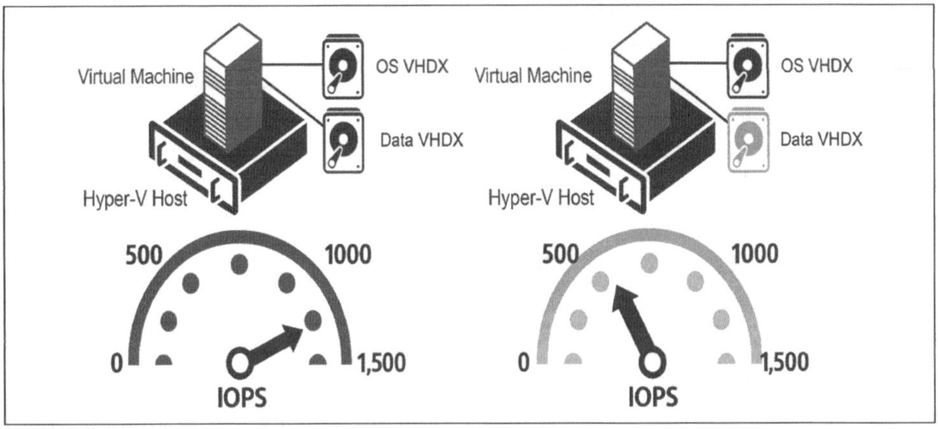

***Fig. 3.27:** IOPS of a Virtual machine*

	Resource	Windows Server 2008 R2 Hyper-V	Windows Server 2012 R2 Hyper-V	Improvement Factor
Host	Logical Processors	64	320	5×
	Physical Memory	1TB	4TB	4×
	Virtual CPUs per Host	512	2,048	4×
VM	Virtual CPUs per VM	4	64	16×
	Memroy per VM	64GB	1TB	16×
	Active VMs per Host	384	1,024	2.7×
	Guest NUMA	No	Yes	,
Cluster	Maximum Nodes	16	64	4×
	Maximum VMs	1,000	8,000	8×

***Fig. 3.28:** Hyper V comparison*

3.12 Virtual Box

Oracle VM VirtualBox is cross platform virtualization software that allows we to extend ourexisting computer to run multiple operating systems at the same time. Designed for IT professionals and developers, Oracle VM VirtualBox runs on Windows, Mac OS X, Linux and Oracle Solaris systems and is ideal for testing, developing, demonstrating and deployingsolutions across multiple platforms on one machine.

Key Benefits

- Run almost any type of application on our existing machine
- Quickly and easily try out new platforms
- Create a multiplatform test and development environment
- Build a multi1tier demonstration system on a single portable machine
- Extend the lifetime and usefulness of existing computers
- Run legacy platforms and applications on modern hardware
- Easily create isolated environments

Key Features

- Available for Windows, Mac OS X, Linux and Oracle Solaris host operating systems (OS)
- Supports a wide range of guest platforms
- Easy to use graphical user interface
- Poourful, scriptable command line interface
- Import and export virtual machines using OVF/OVA standards
- Shared folders between guest and host
- Seamless, resizable, and full screen window display modes
- Video and 3D (OpenGL, DirectX) acceleration
- Virtual webcam
- Multiple virtual screen support
- Poourful and flexible networking options
- USB 1.1/2.0/3.0 and serial ports
- SAS, SATA, SCSI and IDE storage controllers
- Built-in iSCSI initiator
- Built-in Remote Display Server
- Multi-generational branched snapshots
- Linked and full clones
- Controllable copy and paste
- Screen-recording facility
- Disk image encryption
- HiDPI support
- Drag and drop support

3.12.1 Oracle VM VirtualBox Manager Screen

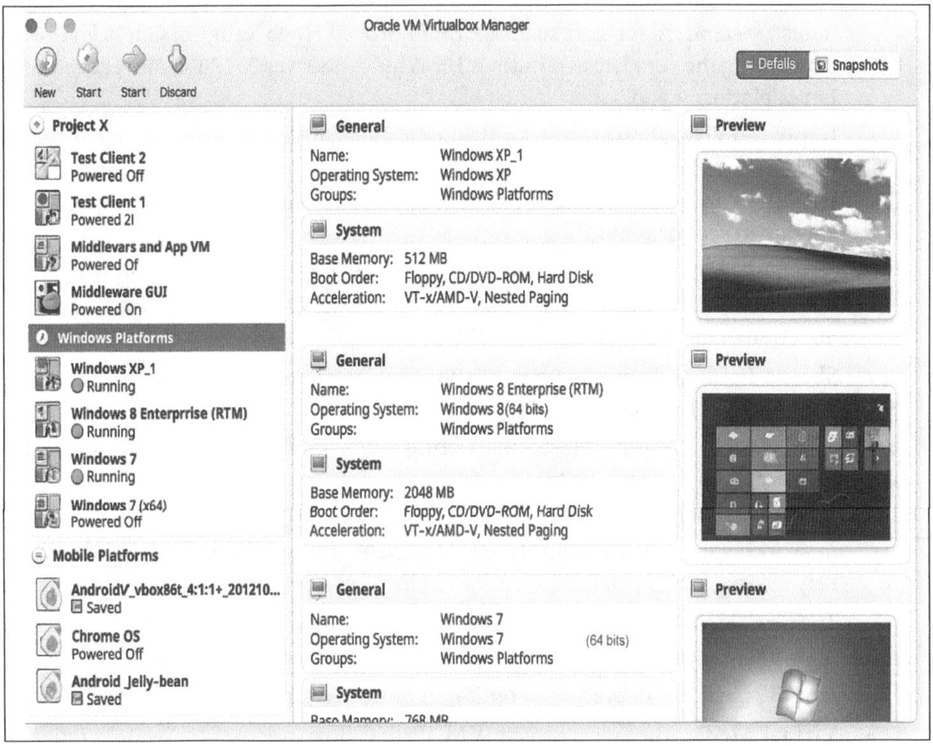

Fig. 3.29: Oracle VM VirtualBox Manager Screen

Easy to Use, Fast and Powerful, Great Platform Coverage

Designed for use on systems ranging from ultrabooks to high end server class hardware, Oracle VM Virtual Box is lightweight and easy to install and use. Yet under the simple exterior lies an extremely fast and poourful virtualization engine.

With a formidable reputation for speed and agility, Oracle VM Virtual Box contains innovative features to deliver tangible business benefits: significant performance improvements; a more poourful virtualization system and a wider range of supported guest operating system platforms.

Easy to Use

Improved Virtual Box Manager with further features – The Oracle VM Virtual Box Managernow supports hot-plug for SATA virtual disks and the option to customize status bar, menu bar and guest-content scaling for each virtual machine deployed;

- **New Introduced Headless and Detachable start options:** The Oracle VM Virtual Box Manager now supports to start virtual machine in the background with a separate frontend process that can be closed while the virtual machine continues to work;
- **Easy to use Wizards:** Wizards help with the creation of new virtual machines. Preconfiguredsettings are used based on the type of guest OS;

- **Easy import and export of appliances:** Virtual machines can be created, configured and thenshared by exporting and importing virtual appliances using industry-standard formats such as.ova; Improved Huge Range of Guest Platforms – including the very latest Windows 10, WindowsServer 2012 R2 and leading edge Linux platforms too.
- **Improved Virtual Box Guest Additions:** Installed inside the guest virtual machine, the GuestAdditions provide a more natural user experience. For example, guest windows can be easilyresized to arbitrary resolutions, made full-screen or even operate in seamless mode.

  And data can be copy and pasted to and from, and between, concurrently running machines and the host platform. This functionality is now controllable as bi-directional, uni-directional, or disabled;
- **Shared Folders:** Share our host platform's filesystem with the guest to facilitate real cross-platform computing;
- **Multi-touch support:** Hosts supporting multi-touch interfaces can now also deliver this to their guests too;
- **Flexible Networking options:** Oracle VM Virtual Box offers a rich range of networking models from easy-to-use NAT networking, to fully functional Bridged networking, and specialist Internal and Host-only networking too.

  The new "NAT Network" mode allows multiple guests to run on the same internal network, seeing each other, and also the outside world via a new NAT service;
- **IPv6:** IPv6 is now offered as an option in most networking modes alongside IPv4;
- **Virtual Media Manager:** Oracle VM Virtual Box supports the widest range of virtual disk formats from its own native. vdi format to those offered by Microsoft (.vhd), VMware (.vmdk), and Parallels (.vdd). The Virtual Media Manager tool now allows conversions between formats using an easy to use graphical user interface;
- **Video Capture:** A built-in recording mechanism of the guest's screen contents. Easy to startand stop, recording one or more virtual screens to the standard webm format.

3.12.2 Performance

- **Improved Latest Intel and AMD hardware support:** Harnessing the latest in chip- level support for virtualization, Oracle VM Virtual Box supports even the most recent AMD and Intel processors bringing faster execution times for everything from Windows to Linux and Oracle Solaris guests. But Virtual Box will also run on older hardware without VT support;
- **Improved Instruction Set extended:** More instruction set extensions available to the guest when running with hardware-assisted virtualization; this include also AES-NI that improve the speed of applications performing encryption and decryption using Advanced EncryptionStandard (AES);
- **New Para virtualization Support:** Virtual Box allows exposing a para-virtualization interfaceto facilitate accurate and efficient execution of software by leveraging built- in virtualizationsupport of modern Linux and Microsoft Windows;

- **New Disk Image Encryption:** Virtual Box allows to encrypt data stored in hard disk imagestransparently for the guest. Virtual Box uses the AES algorithm and supports 128 or 256-bitdata encryption keys;
- **Improved Bi-Directional Drag and Drop support:** On all host platforms, Windows, Linux and Oracle Solaris guests now support "drag and drop" of content between the host and the guest.

  The drag and drop feature transparently allows copying or opening of files, directories,and more;
- **High-performance storage I/O subsystem:** Oracle VM Virtual Box offers a wide range of virtual storage controllers including SAS, SATA, SCSI and IDE controllers. Virtual Box utilizes an asynchronous I/O virtual disk subsystem to achieve high-performance whilst maintaining high data integrity;
- **Built-in iSCSI Initiator:** Oracle VM Virtual Box includes an iSCSI initiator that allows virtual disks to exist as iSCSI targets. The guest sees a standard storage controller but disk accesses are translated into iSCSI commands and sent across the network;
- **3D graphics and video acceleration:** The Guest Additions feature new, improved display drivers that accelerate 3D graphics by intercepting OpenGL and Direct3D calls in the guest and leveraging the host's GPU to render the images and video onto the screen.
- **Remote Display Protocol:** The unique built-in Virtual Box Remote Display Protocol (VRDP) enables poourful remote, graphical access to the console of the guest. Microsoft RDP capable clients can connect to one or more remote monitors, with USB deviceredirection when using rdesktop-based clients. VRDP is now also accessible over IPv6;
- **Improved Serial and USB connections:** External devices can be connected to guests, with specific USB devices selected by a poourful filter mechanism; now Virtual Box supports upto USB 3.0 devices;
- **Virtual webcam:** On hosts with cameras, Virtual Box now exposes a virtual webcam allowing guests running apps such as Skype or Google Hangouts to use the host camera;
- **High-Definition audio:** Guests enjoy the rich audio capabilities of an Intel high definition audio card;
- **Full ACPI support:** The host's poour status is fully available to the guest and ACPI button events can be sent to the guest to control the lifecycle of the virtual machine;
- **Linked and full clones:** Oracle VM Virtual Box makes it easy to clone virtual machines. Clones can be full copies of configuration information and virtual disks, or may share a parentvirtual disk for faster cloning and greater storage efficiency;
- **Multi-generational and branched snapshots:** Snapshots allow a user to revert to previous known states. Take a snapshot before installing software, then revert to the snapshot to recover the pre-installation state;
- **Page Fusion:** Traditional Page Sharing techniques have suffered from long and expensive cache construction as pages are scrutinized as candidates for de-duplication.

- Taking a smarter approach, Virtual Box Page Fusion uses intelligence in the guest virtual machine to determine much more rapidly and accurately those pages which can be eliminatedthereby increasing the capacity or VM density of the system;
- **Resource controls:** Host resources such as CPU execution, disk and network I/O can be capped or throttled to protect against rogue guests consuming excessive amounts;
- **Guest automation:** The guest automation APIs have been extended to allow host-based logicto drive operations in the guest including update of the Guest Additions;
- **Web services:** A Web service API enables remote control of Virtual Box by authorized clients.

Platforms

- **Commercially supported platforms:** Oracle VM Virtual Box enables we to install and run ahuge range of host and guest platforms. Oracle offers commercial support for the most popular guest operating systems, assuring customers of expert help when they need it.
- **New Oracle Linux 7:** Support for the latest version of Oracle's flagship Linux platform; New Ubuntu and Fedora: Support for both the desktop and server versions of the most popular Ubuntu Linux and Fedora distributions; New Mac OS X 10.10 "Yosemite" – The latest Mac OS X platform from Apple.

3.13 The Eucalyptus Open-Source Private Cloud

Eucalyptus is a Linux-based open-source software architecture that implements efficiency-enhancing private and hybrid clouds within an enterprise's existing IT infrastructure. Eucalyptus is an acronym for "Elastic Utility Computing Architecture for Linking Our Programs to Useful Systems." A Eucalyptus private cloud is deployed across an enterprise's "on premise" data center infrastructure and is accessed by users over enterprise intranet. Thus, sensitive data remains entirely secure from external intrusion behind the enterprise firewall.

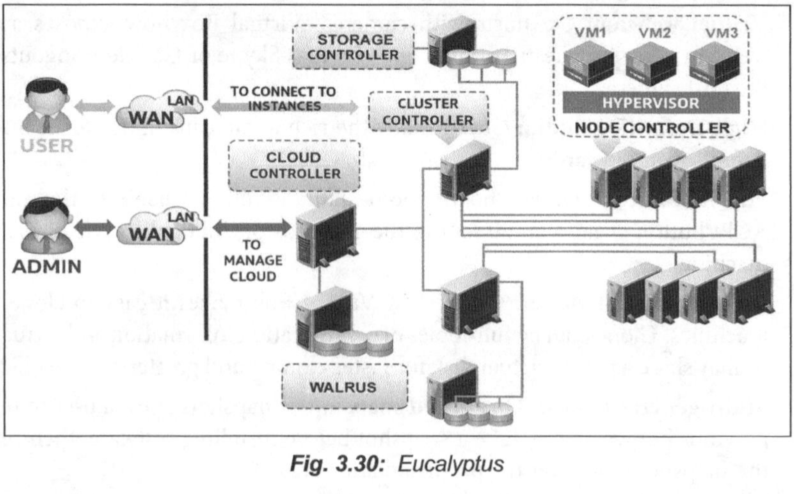

Fig. 3.30: Eucalyptus

Initially developed to support the high performance computing (HPC) research of Professor Rich Wolski's research group at the University of California, Santa Barbara,

Eucalyptus is engineered according to design principles that ensure compatibility with existing Linux- based data center installations. Eucalyptus can be deployed without modification on all major Linux OS distributions, including Ubuntu, RHEL, Centos, and Debian. And Ubuntu distributions now include the Eucalyptus software core as the key component of the Ubuntu Enterprise Cloud.

Eucalyptus Components

Each Eucalyptus service component exposes a well-defined language agnostic API in the form of a WSDL document containing both the operations that the service can perform and the input/output data structures. Inter-service authentication is handled via standard WS- Security mechanisms. There are five high-level components, each with its own Web-serviceinterface, that comprise a Eucalyptus installation. A brief description of the components within the Eucalyptus system follows.

EXERCISE

A. Subjective Questions

1. How does a hybrid cloud offer benefits over private and public clouds?
2. What factors should be considered when choosing a cloud deployment model?
3. Why is virtualization considered a key technology in cloud computing?
4. What are the benefits and limitations of virtualization?
5. Describe different types of virtualization with examples.
6. How does server virtualization improve resource utilization?
7. What is operating system virtualization, and how does it work?
8. How does OS virtualization enhance security and performance in cloud computing?
9. How does KVM differ from other hypervisors like VMware and Hyper-V?
10. What are the main differences between a system VM and a process VM?
11. What is a Virtual Machine Monitor (VMM), and what are its key functions?
12. Explain the different types of Virtual Machine Monitors.
13. Define a hypervisor and explain its importance in virtualization.
14. Compare Type 1 and Type 2 hypervisors with examples.
15. What is Xen Hypervisor, and how does it support cloud computing?
16. How does Xen Hypervisor differ from VMware ESXi?
17. Compare Hyper-V with other hypervisors like Xen and VirtualBox.
18. What is VirtualBox, and how is it used in virtualization?
19. How does Eucalyptus compare to OpenStack as a private cloud solution?

B. Objective Questions

1. What is the first step in deploying an application on the cloud?
   (a) Choosing a cloud service provider (b) Running the application locally
   (c) Writing the code in assembly language (d) Disconnecting from the internet

2. Which of the following cloud service models is commonly used for deploying applications?
   (a) SaaS (b) IaaS
   (c) PaaS (d) All of the above
3. Why is virtualization important in cloud computing?
   (a) It increases hardware dependency
   (b) It allows multiple virtual machines to run on a single physical machine
   (c) It decreases resource efficiency
   (d) It eliminates the need for security
4. Which of the following is NOT a benefit of virtualization?
   (a) Cost reduction (b) Improved scalability
   (c) Increased hardware dependence (d) Enhanced resource utilization
5. Which type of virtualization allows multiple operating systems to run on a single hardware system?
   (a) Network Virtualization (b) Storage Virtualization
   (c) Server Virtualization (d) Application Virtualization
6. Which of the following enables multiple operating systems to run on a single physical machine?
   (a) Hypervisor (b) Load Balancer
   (c) Firewall (d) Database Management System
7. What is KVM in virtualization?
   (a) A hardware component (b) A type of cloud storage
   (c) A Linux-based hypervisor (d) A networking tool
9. What is the role of a Virtual Machine Monitor (VMM)?
   (a) It acts as an interface between hardware and virtual machines
   (b) It manages cloud storage
   (c) It controls internet access
   (d) It is used for database management
10. What is the primary function of a hypervisor?
   (a) Managing virtual machines (b) Storing cloud data
   (c) Encrypting network traffic (d) Hosting websites
11. Which cloud providers use Xen Hypervisor?
   (a) AWS and Oracle Cloud (b) Google Drive and Dropbox
   (c) Microsoft Office and Gmail (d) None of the above
12. Hyper-V is developed by which company?
   (a) Google (b) Microsoft
   (c) IBM (d) Apple

UNIT 4

Management in Cloud Computing and Security

4.1 Cloud Data Centers

A data center (or datacenter) is a facility composed of networked computers and storage that businesses or other organizations use to organize, process, store and disseminate large amounts of data. A business typically relies heavily upon the applications, services and data contained within a data center, making it a focal point and critical asset for everyday operations.

Data centers are not a single thing, but rather, a conglomeration of elements. At a minimum, data centers serve as the principal repositories for all manner of IT equipment, including servers, storage subsystems, networking switches, routers and firewalls, as well as the cabling and physical racks used to organize and interconnect the IT equipment. A data center must also contain an adequate infrastructure, such as power distribution and supplemental power subsystems, including electrical switching; uninterruptible power supplies; backup generators and so on; ventilation and data center cooling systems, such as computer room air conditioners; and adequate provisioning for network carrier (telco) connectivity. All of this demands a physical facility with physical security and sufficient physical space to house the entire collection of infrastructure and equipment.

4.1.1 Data Center Consolidation and Collocation

There is no requirement for a single data center, and modern businesses may use two or more data center installations across multiple locations for greater resilience and better application performance, which lowers latency by locating workloads closer to users.

Conversely, a business with multiple data centers may opt to consolidate data centers, reducing the number of locations in order to minimize the costs of IT operations. Consolidation typically occurs during mergers and acquisitions when the majority business doesn't need the data centers owned by the subordinate business. Alternatively, data center operators can pay a fee to rent server space and other hardware in a co location facility. Co-location is an appealing option for organizations that want to avoid the large capital expenditures associated with building and maintaining their own data centers.

Today, co-location providers are expanding their offerings to include managed services, such as inter-connectivity, allowing customers to connect to the public cloud.

4.1.2. Data Center Tiers

Data centers are not defined by their physical size or style. Small businesses may operate successfully with several servers and storage arrays networked within a convenient closet or small room, while major computing organizations, such as Facebook, Amazon or Google, may fill an enormous warehouse space with data center equipment and infrastructure. In other cases, data centers can be assembled in mobile installations, such as shipping containers, also known as data centers in a box, which can be moved and deployed as required.

However, data centers can be defined by various levels of reliability or resilience, sometimes referred to as data center tiers. In 2005, the American National Standards Institute (ANSI) and the Telecommunications Industry Association (TIA) published standard ANSI/TIA-942, "Telecommunications Infrastructure Standard for Data Centers," which defined four tiers of data center design and implementation guidelines. Each subsequent tier is intended to provide more resilience, security and reliability than the previous tier. For example, a tier 1 data center is little more than a server room, while a tier 4 data center offers redundant subsystems and high security.

4.1.3 Data Center Architecture and Design

Although almost any suitable space could conceivably serve as a "data center," the deliberate design and implementation of a data center requires careful consideration. Beyond the basic issues of cost and taxes, sites are selected based on a multitude of criteria, such as geographic location, seismic and meteorological stability, access to roads and airports, availability of energy and telecommunications and even the prevailing political environment.

Once a site is secured, the data center architecture can be designed with attention to the mechanical and electrical infrastructure, as well as the composition and layout of the IT equipment. All of these issues are guided by the availability and efficiency goals of the desired data center tier.

4.2 Energy Consumption and Efficiency

Data center designs also recognize the importance of energy efficiency. A simple data center may need only a few kilowatts of energy, but an enterprise-scale data center installation can demand tens of megawatts or more. Today, the green data center, which is designed for minimum environmental impact through the use of low-emission building materials, catalytic converters and alternative energy technologies, is growing in popularity.

Organizations often measure data center energy efficiency through a metric called power usage effectiveness (PUE), which represents the ratio of total power entering the data center divided by the power used by IT equipment. However, the subsequent rise of virtualizationhas allowed for much more productive use of IT equipment, resulting in much higher efficiency, lower energy use and energy cost mitigation. Metrics such as PUE are no longer central to energy efficiency goals, but organizations may still gauge PUE and employ comprehensive power and cooling analyses to better understand and manage energy efficiency.

Data center designs must also implement sound safety and security practices. For example, safety is often reflected in the layout of doorways and access corridors, which must accommodate the movement of large, unwieldy IT equipment, as well as permit employees to access and repair the infrastructure. Fire suppression is another key safety area, and the extensive use of sensitive, high- energy electrical and electronic equipment precludes common sprinklers. Instead, data centers often use environmentally friendly chemical fire suppression systems, which effectively starve a fire of oxygen while mitigating collateral damage to the equipment. Since the data center is also a core business asset, comprehensive security measures, like badge access and video surveillance, help to detect and prevent malfeasance by employees, contractors and intruders.

4.2.1 Data Center Infrastructure Management and Monitoring

Modern data centers make extensive use of monitoring and management software. Software such as data center infrastructure management tools allow remote IT administrators to oversee the facility and equipment, measure performance, detect failures and implement a wide array of corrective actions, without ever physically entering the data center room.

The growth of virtualization has added another important dimension to data center infrastructure management. Virtualization now supports the abstraction of servers, networks and storage, allowing every computing resource to be organized into pools without regard to their physical location. Administrators can then provision workloads, storage instances and even network configuration from those common resource pools. When administrators no longer need those resources, they can return them to the pool for reuse. All of these actions can be implemented through software, giving traction to the term software-defined data center.

4.2.2 Data Center vs. Cloud

Data centers are increasingly implementing private cloud software, which builds on virtualization to add a level of automation, user self-service and billing/chargeback to data center administration. The goal is to allow individual users to provision workloads and other computing resources on- demand, without IT administrative intervention.

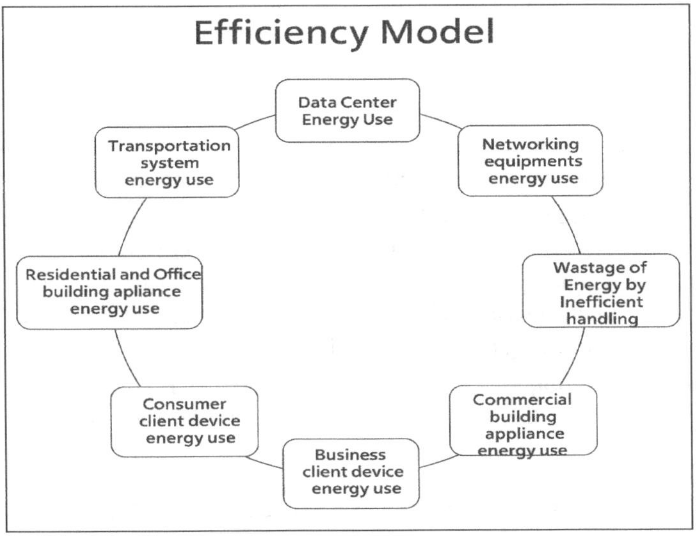

Fig. 4.1: Efficiency Model

It is also increasingly possible for data centers to interface with public cloud providers. Platforms such as Microsoft Azure emphasize the hybrid use of local data centers with Azure or other public cloud resources. The result is not an elimination of data centers, but rather, the creation of a dynamic environment that allows organizations to run workloads locally or in the cloud or to move those instances to or from the cloud as desired.

Fig. 4.2: Mobile Cloud

Mobile Cloud Computing, or MCC, merges the fast-growing Cloud Computing Applications market with the ubiquitous smartphone. One of the most ground-breaking blends of modern-day technologies, MCC has proved itself to be highly beneficial to all the mobile users and cloud-based service-providers as well.

In this technique, user-friendly mobile applications are developed, which are powered by and hosted using the cloud computing technology. The 'mobile cloud' approach enables theapps. Developers to build applications designed especially for mobile-users, which can be used without being bound to the operating system of the device or its capacity to store data. Here, the tasks of data-processing and data storage are performed outside the mobile devices.

The ability of MCC to allow the device to run cloud-based web-applications unlike other native apps differentiates it from the concept of 'Mobile Computing'. Here the users can remotely access the store applications and their associated data anytime on the Internet by subscribing to the cloud services. Although most devices already run a mix of web-based and native apps, the trend these days seems to be shifting more toward the services and convenience that are offered by a mobile cloud.

Researchers are putting in serious efforts in forming a strong and symbiotic platform, coined the 'Third Platform,' that would bring together the mobile and the cloud. Experts predict this platform to revolutionize further the uprising of MCC which has enabled its users a better means to access and store their data along with latest data synchronization techniques,improved reliability and better performance. All these beneficial aspects have inspired a lot of people to consider MCC for their smart-phones.

Mobile Cloud Computing confirms the impact of certain trends and factors. Here are the factors that have had an astounding impact as far as MCC is concerned.

- **Enhanced broadband coverage:** Better connectivity is being rendered to our mobile devices via 4G, WiFi, femto-cells, fixed wireless etc.
- **Abundant Storage:** Cloud-based mobile apps have proved themselves to be more capable than any smart-phone, especially in terms of the storage space that is offered. Cloud apps' server- based computing infrastructure that is accessible through mobile interface of an app, is quite a contrast to the limited data-storage space and processing power in a mobile device.
- **Budding Technologies:** Advanced technologies like HTML5, CSS3, Hyper-Visor virtual machines for smart-phones, cloudlets and Web 4.0 etc are contributing a lot toward MCC's rising popularity.

4.3 Data Management in Cloud Computing

Data is born around us to evolve every second. This process promises the ability to return anywhere, anytime but the information must also be protected properly with the help of the right data management solution. Some people may experience difficulties in deciding how to start working in the cloud or fail to recognize those promised benefits while on their way. Although the cloud does not come with an instruction manual, it can work for you and your business, anyway. All you need is to have your data managed well.

Businesses used to have centralized on-premise data warehouses where information was safe. Yet, as time went by, it became harder to maintain them; highly skilled manpower and greater maintenance fees are needed now. So, now, in our cloud age, when people are willing to access their data easily, an innovative management solution is what can help extract the full value of data to put it to good use. Management methods applied to data that is stored in the cloud differ from the traditional ones since cloud data analytics has to meet the requirements of enhanced cloud data security and integrity.

4.3.1 Data Management Strategy in Cloud Computing

Data migration to the cloud is the real deal that requires a holistic approach. This process is oftentimes hard. Therefore, it is the primary objectives of your business that should dictate your strategy in the first place. Positive changes are incremental and no miracle will happen once you start, not to mention the fact that data management is continuous and must be constantly monitored after the strategic planning is done.

One of the most undesirable effects of the wrong data management strategy that everybody stands a hazard to experience is a substantial increase in costs. Due to the growing complexity of cloud-driven environments, enterprises expenditures can be unreasonably high. Nonetheless, you can control a budgeting process and do not have to spend as much as one used to when there was a need for costly servers and systems. Accordingly, developing an effective strategy to minimize the number of obstacles you might face by considering its key elements is critical for you. These aspects are the following:

1. A Systematic Approach to Data Security

Overcoming and preventing security challenges should be a data management system's primary concern. Firewalls, data encryption, and data exposure are some possible protective measures. More stringent control is needed for ensuring security in the cloud. Thus, data governance must be standardized within your enterprise for your data to be secured at rest, in flight or when going outside the production environment. Make sure you have considered and employed all possible security cloud services that can help you detect and respond to threats and actual leakages. Then, it will be easier to comply with existing data management policies.

2. Tiers optimization for Specific Workloads

Tiering is, in the first place, meant to add efficiency to your data management strategy, derive value from and add value to your data. With the tiered storage, frequently accessed objects will be stored in higher-performing storage pools while the more rarely accessed data objects whose volume is bigger will be stored in larger-capacity storage pools. Besides, your data will be structured, which means lower latency.

3. Flexibility in Managing Multi-Structured Data

Multi-structured data make up separate sets of data managed and stored in multiple formats. So, it is easy to overspend on storage and analytics. Nevertheless, it is the unified data management that affords flexibility, operational and cost efficiency in your cloud data analytics.

4.4 Mistakes to be Avoided in Cloud Management Systems

Now that we have highlighted three pillars that your data migration strategy must rest upon, it is time to define data management challenges in cloud computing and the potential risk factors that may hinder your efforts.

1. No Corporate Policy

Any strategic initiative, especially the one that is process-centric, has to comply with the corresponding policies and standards. Essentially, data management is the tactical execution thereof and a good idea here is to consolidate as many entities as possible into one system. Then, one will not only be able to manage data at lower costs but will also do it more securely. Data that is kept separately and managed in several different ways within one organization can be easy to access and control can be provided at the insufficient quality. Centralized and consistent policies will result in making more right decisions and fewer mistakes.

2. Moving All Your Data to the Cloud

Despite all those great things about cloud computing, enterprises should never forget about the local file servers, domain controllers and the value they add to your solution. Data-driven decisions can still be made without driving all you have to the cloud. First, one has to think over what information can stay in an on-premise server and what should go to a cloud server for further processing.

3. Limited Structure

Data must be structured. When it is organized, it is accessible and you do not have to waste your time on searching. Thus, proper classification and strict formats for document names are essential.

4.5 Best Practices for Data Management in Cloud Computing

If there are core principles that lay the foundation for the strategic management of data in the cloud and certain pitfalls to avoid, then there must be methods and techniques that are, if compared with the traditional ones, aimed at the operational excellence and overall improvement of your experience.

1. Ensure a sophisticated infrastructure. Everything will work smoothly and efficiently if there is a possibility to choose whether you want to move data to on-prem storages, to the cloud, or across different clouds. The cloud is not the only destination of a mass data migration. The structure has to be sophisticated yet this whole system should have centralized management.
2. Choose your cloud data management platform. Platforms like this are used for control, monitoring and other relevant cloud activities. Modern enterprises tend to constantly change their IT environments by making them larger and more complex. If you do provide such an infrastructure managing different types of data across various cloud computing services and local servers, then selecting a single platform is highly recommended. This platform approach will help you maintain a certain level of consistency and reduce bottlenecks. Besides you can opt for a platform that is native, cloud provider-specific, or available from a third-party vendor.
3. Leverage the Cloud Data Management Interface. It is a generally accepted standard of interface's functioning which allows enterprises to manage data elements increasing the system's interoperability. Accommodation of requirements from multiple vendors instead of using the storage system with a unique interface

might be challenging, so the deployment of CDMI compatible systems is the right thing to do.

4. Create a framework for cloud management first. Before moving data to the cloud, make sure there is a solid framework. Upon having one established, it will be easier for an enterprise to say how to best manage its cloud resources. Migration of systems to more capable platforms is a natural process, but it has to be a conscious and informed decision.

4.6 Cloud data management trends

Watching for the trends in the field you are professionally involved in is extremely welcome. Although cloud computing is in itself a trend, there is also a general course of action that emphasizes the importance of effective cloud data management. Accordingly, trends in managing data in the cloud can be further subdivided to include the following:

1. The number of enterprises leveraging multiple data centers that work and is managed as one large entity is increasing.
2. Businesses are reviewing their cloud data management strategies. Now, to drive business decisions, they want to know more about their growing data volumes.

Infrastructures are modernized to support digital technologies like Artificial Intelligence and Machine Learning that will deliver insights to guide decision-making and manage the increased workloads effectively.

Corporate data is going to exist in so many different places as never before including the cloud and "as-a-service" applications.

Enterprises have to comply with and understand more requirements and policies. No matter how big the company is, it has to ensure data governance policies are in place before migrating data.large capital expenditures associated with building and maintaining their own data centers. Today, colocation providers are expanding their offerings to include managed services, such as interconnectivity, allowing customers to connect to the public cloud.

4.7 Data Center Security and Safety

Data center designs must also implement sound safety and security practices. For example, safety is often reflected in the layout of doorways and access corridors, which must accommodate the movement of large, unwieldy IT equipment, as well as permit employees to access and repair the infrastructure. Fire suppression is another key safety area, and the extensive use of sensitive, high- energy electrical and electronic equipment precludes common sprinklers. Instead, data centers often use environmentally friendly chemical fire suppression systems, which effectively starve a fire of oxygen while mitigating collateral damage to the equipment. Since the data center is also a core business asset, comprehensive security measures, like badge access and video surveillance, help to detect and prevent malfeasance by employees, contractors and intruders.

Mobile cloud computing uses cloud computing to deliver applications to mobile devices. These mobile apps can be deployed remotely using speed and flexibility and development tools. Mobile cloud applications can be built or revised quickly using cloud services. They can be delivered to many different devices with different operating systems, computing tasks, and data storage. Thus, users can access applications that could not otherwise be supported.

4.8 Open Source and Commercial Clouds

With so many open-source and commercial tools available for cloud management, how do you, as an IT operations management professional, decide which is the best fit for your team's needs? Here's a quick rundown of the general strengths and weaknesses of open-source versus commercial tool options, and when it makes sense to have one, the other, or a mix.

You need a plan for where free and open-source tools fit into your overall cloud management strategy, and where you should consider commercial options to complete the picture and meet your overall needs.

Here's how to get started.

But IT is missing out on something when it chooses to go exclusively on the open-source route. Organizations that have a religious commitment to open source risk having the pendulum swing to far in that direction. Open source doesn't solve all problems, so it's important to keep traditional software options in the mix when considering your cloud management tool needs. Open-source is an option, not a religion

People like to get by with open source, and they also like the fact that they can have a greater influence on the maturation of open-source tools. Many companies' dedication to the open- source concept is almost religious.

While cloud management and monitoring platforms provide very different types of capabilities, a good depiction of common patterns appears in Figure 1 below. Keep in mind that humans sit at the highest level in this stack, since they provide core monitoring services. However, there is also automation at this level, meaning that you can set up rules and policies that can take automatic corrective action.

One example is the ability to automatically provision more virtual storage when a database is about to run out of space. Another is the ability to provision more machine instances when performance starts to lag. It's helpful to look at the realities of both types of software, open source and commercial, when it comes to cloud management tools. Both approaches have pros and cons.

The upside is that it's free, and can be had for the price of a download from GitHub or another open-source download site. Moreover, you don't need to go through hours and hours of meeting with vendors, as well as the drudgery of enterprise software negotiations. You need it, you download it, you install it, and you're ready to test or deploy.

Another pro is that you have a say in how the product matures over time. These are community-driven projects, and you can contribute to the code tree and make recommendations as to the software's direction. The downside is that you have to pay people to do that on behalf of your business, and there's an opportunity cost to that. Is there a return on investment for your business to advance the software or add a key new feature?

On the downside, open source, generally speaking, is not as mature as commercial offerings. In general, you'll experience more problems with open-source cloud management software, and you'll have to deal with those problems yourself, working with the community—or by engaging a company that provides consulting services around its distribution of an open source cloud management system.

Second, bug fixes and new features may take months—or years—to show up in the core code tree. This is due largely to the fact that volunteers make the fixes and/or enhancements. This lack of a profit motive can significantly delay releases compared to the commercial world, where money talks and motivates the cloud management provider to make the fixes and improvements you've requested as soon as possible.

4.9 Cloud simulator

Coud computing provides all kind of computational services like scalability, resource provisioning, security, fault tolerance and sustainability etc. To ensure the applicability of all these characteristics, it is required to evaluate cloud applications before implementing or deploying it in real world. The main reason behind this is that it is quite difficult to alter the limitations occurred during executing in real time. It may lead to overhead of provider, increased costs and wastage of time. Simulation is the best method to avoid all these kind of frustrations. The very first simulation tool CloudSim was released in the year of 2009 by Cloud Computing and Distributed Systems (CLOUDS) Laboratory, at the Computer Science and Software Engineering Department of the University of Melbourne. Succeeding CloudSim, many other simulators such as CloudAnalyst, EmuSim, DCSim, iCanCloudhave evolved gradually to ease the implementation of custom applications.

The CloudSim Simulator

CloudSim is the basic simulation tool that provides provision to implement the custom applications and hence the motivation to adopt this tool for the current research works. Various versions of CloudSim have been released since 2009.

4.9.1 Architecture of CloudSim

CloudSimfollows the layered architecture.As is clear from the figure, the architecture mainly comprises of threelayers specifically user code, components of CloudSim and the simulation engine. It provides the full virtualized environment along with keen interface for virtual machine services, cloud services and network. Each of the components is briefly described as follows:

This section consists of simulation specifications and scheduling policy. It interpretsthe basic entities for hosting like virtual machines, VM configurations, VM requirements, number of users and scheduling processes.Using these configurations the cloud developer can deploy the federated clouds and implement the custom application of resource provisioning and load distribution.

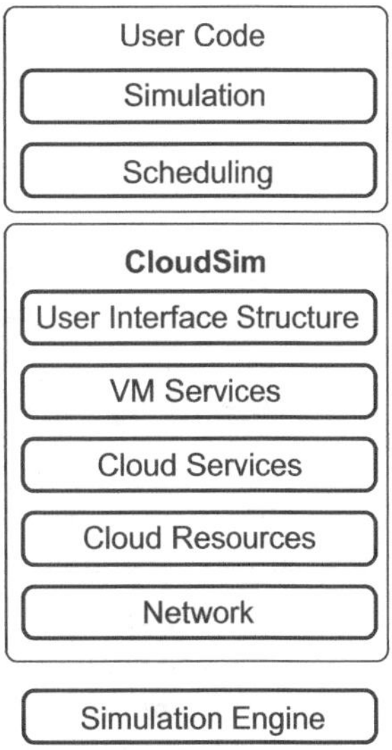

Fig. 4.3: Architecture of CloudSim

4.10 Sensor-Cloud

Sensor-Cloud is a new paradigm for cloud computing that uses the physical sensors to accumulate its data and transmit all sensor data into a cloud computing infrastructure. Sensor-Cloud handles sensor data efficiently, which is used for many monitoring applications. Sensor-Cloud is a new paradigm for cloud computing that uses the physical sensors to accumulate its data and transmit all sensor data into a cloud computing infrastructure. Sensor- Cloud handles sensor data efficiently, which is used for many monitoring applications.

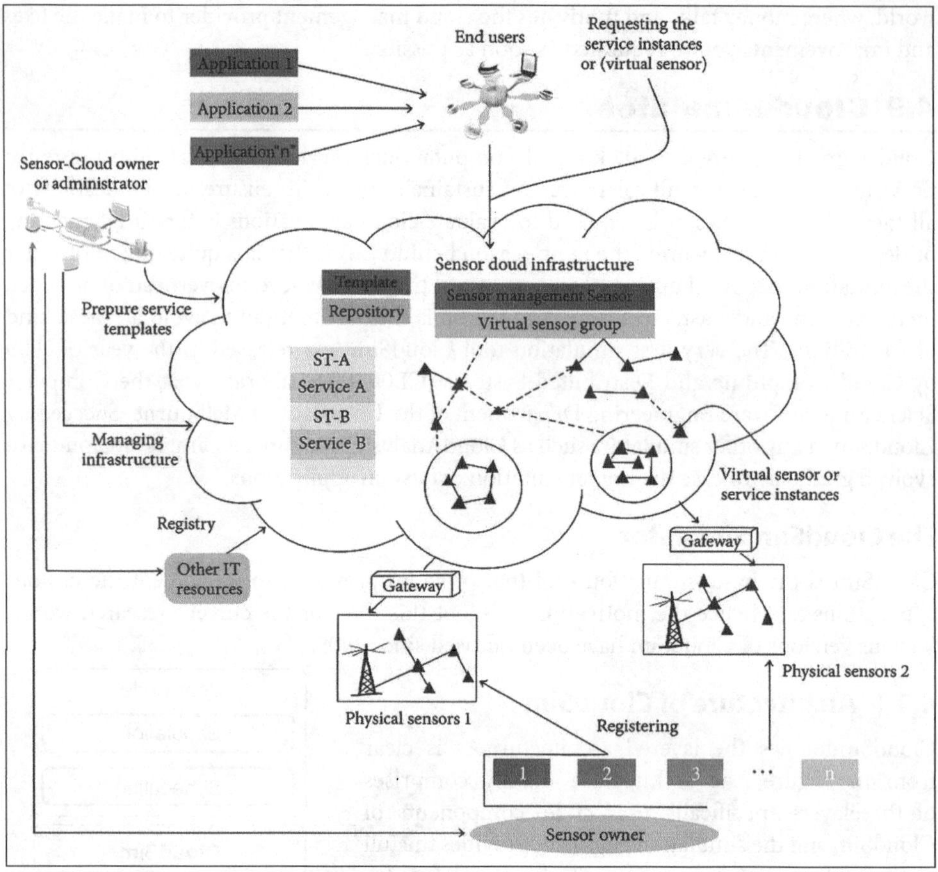

Fig. 4.4: Architecture of Sensor-Cloud

Description of Sensor Cloud

- **Analysis:** The integration of huge accumulated sensor data from several sensor networks and the cloud computing model make it attractive for various kinds of analyses required by users through provisioning of the scalable processing.
- **Scalability:** Sensor-Cloud enables the earlier sensor networks to scale on very large size because of the large routing architecture of cloud. It means that as the need for resources increases, organizations can scale or add the extra services from cloud computing vendors without having to invest heavily for these additional hardware resources.
- **Collaboration:** Sensor-Cloud enables the huge sensor data to be shared by different groups of consumers through collaboration of various physical sensor networks. It eases the collaboration among several users and applications for huge data sharing on the cloud.
- **Visualization:** Sensor-Cloud platform provide a visualization API to be used for representing the diagrams with the stored and retrieved sensor data from several device assets. Through the visualization tools, users can predict the possible future trends that have to be incurred.

- **Free Provisioning of Increased Data storage and Processing Power:** It provides free data storage and organizations may put their data rather than putting onto private computer systems without hassle. It provides enormous processing facility and storage resources to handle data of large-scale applications.
- **Dynamic Provisioning of Services:** Users of Sensor-Cloud can access their relevant information from wherever they want and whenever they need rather than being stick to their desks.
- **Multitenancy:** The number of services from several service providers can be integrated easily through cloud and Internet for numerous service innovations to meet user's demand. Sensor-Cloud allows the accessibility to several numbers of data centers placed anywhere on the network world.
- **Automation:** Automation played a vital role in provisioning of Sensor-Cloud computing services. Automation of services improved the delivery time to a great extent.
- **Flexibility:** Sensor-Cloud provides more flexibility to its users than the past computing methods. It provides flexibility to use random applications in any number of times and allows sharing of sensor resources under flexible usage environment.
- **Agility of Services:** Sensor-Cloud provides agile services and the users can provision the expensive technological infrastructure resources with less cost. The integration of wireless sensor networks with cloud allows the high-speed processing of data using immense processing capability of cloud.
- **Resource Optimization:** Sensor-Cloud infrastructure enables the resource optimization by allowing the sharing of resources for several number of applications. The integration of sensors with cloud enables gradual reduction of resource cost and achieves higher gains of services. With Sensor-Cloud, both the small and midsized organizations can benefit from an enormous resource infrastructure without having to involve and administer it directly.
- **Quick Response Time:** The integration of WSN's with cloud provides a very quick response to the user, that is, in real-time due to the large routing architecture of cloud. The quick response time of data feeds from several sensor networks or devices allows users to make critical decisions in near real time.

4.11 Cloud Security

Cloud security is the protection of data, applications, and infrastructures involved in cloud computing. Many aspects of security for cloud environments (whether it's a public, private, or hybridcloud) are the same as for any on-premise IT architecture.

High-level security concerns—like unauthorized data exposure and leaks, weak access controls, susceptibility to attacks, and availability disruptions—affect traditional IT and cloud systems alike. Like any computing environment, cloud security involves maintaining adequate preventative protections.

- Know that the data and systems are safe.
- Can see the current state of security.
- Know immediately if anything unusual happens.
- Can trace and respond to unexpected events.

4.12 Storage Security

Storage security is the collective processes, tools and technologies that ensure that only authorized and legitimate users store, access and use storage resources. It enables better security of any storage resource through the implementation of required technologies and policies on storage access and consumption and the denial of access to all unidentified and potentially malicious users.

Storage security is a broad term that encompasses the implementation and management of security across all layers of a storage environment. This includes storage hardware, software, networks and/or the physical security of storage resources. Typically, storage security primarily deals with implementation at the software or logical layer. This is achieved through several

Techniques such as encrypting/encoding data at rest and in motion, firewalling storage servers and implementing enterprise-wide identity and access management (IAM). Besides individuals, storage security also encompasses the management and protection of storage resources from unverified applications and services.

EXERCISE

A. Objective Questions

1. What is the primary purpose of a cloud data center?
   (a) Storing physical documents
   (b) Hosting applications and data storage
   (c) Printing and scanning services
   (d) Manufacturing hardware
2. Which of the following is a key benefit of data center consolidation?
   (a) Increased energy consumption (b) Higher operational costs
   (c) Reduced IT footprint and efficiency (d) Slower processing speeds
3. Data Center Tiers define:
   (a) The number of users accessing the cloud
   (b) Levels of reliability and uptime availability
   (c) Storage capacity in a data center
   (d) Types of data stored in a cloud
4. What does collocation in data centers refer to?
   (a) Hosting IT infrastructure in a third-party data center
   (b) Using multiple clouds simultaneously
   (c) Storing backup data in-house
   (d) Running a cloud system without virtualization
5. What is a primary concern in data center energy efficiency?
   (a) High hardware failure rates (b) Increased power consumption
   (c) Excess storage capacity (d) Lack of networking infrastructure

6. Which of the following is a critical data management strategy in cloud computing?
   (a) Manual data entry
   (b) Automated backup and recovery
   (c) Ignoring data encryption
   (d) Using only on-premises storage
7. What is one of the biggest mistakes to avoid in cloud data management?
   (a) Implementing multi-layer security
   (b) Using encryption for sensitive data
   (c) Failing to monitor data compliance and security
   (d) Regularly backing up cloud data
8. Which of the following is a best practice for cloud data management?
   (a) Storing all data in a single location
   (b) Implementing access control policies
   (c) Ignoring compliance regulations
   (d) Disabling automatic data backups
9. What is a cloud simulator used for?
   (a) Physical construction of cloud data centers
   (b) Simulating cloud environments for testing and research
   (c) Increasing real-time cloud performance
   (d) Reducing storage space in data centers
10. Open-source clouds like OpenStack are preferred because:
   (a) They are proprietary and expensive
   (b) They allow customization and cost-effectiveness
   (c) They do not support large-scale enterprises
   (d) They restrict multi-cloud environments

B. Subjective Questions

1. What are cloud data centers, and how do they differ from traditional data centers?
2. Explain the importance of data center consolidation and its impact on cloud efficiency.
3. Describe the different tiers of a data center and their role in cloud computing.
4. What are the key data management strategies used in cloud environments?
5. Discuss the common mistakes organizations make in cloud data management systems.
6. Explain best practices for ensuring secure and efficient cloud data management.
7. What are the primary security risks in cloud data centers, and how can they be mitigated?
8. Compare open-source vs. commercial cloud solutions, highlighting their advantages and disadvantages.
9. Describe the role of cloud simulators in cloud research and testing.
10. Explain the architecture of CloudSim and how it helps in simulating cloud environments.
11. What are the challenges of multi-cloud environments, and how can organizations manage them effectively?

Intentionally Left Blank!

UNIT 5

Fog Computing

5.1 Fog Computing

Fog computing is a decentralized computing infrastructure or process in which computing resources are located between the data source and the cloud or any other data center. Fog computing is a paradigm that provides services to user requests at the edge networks. The devices at the fog layer usually perform operations related to networking such as routers, gateways, bridges, and hubs. Researchers envision these devices to be capable of performing both computational and networking operations, simultaneously. Although these devices are resource-constrained compared to the cloud servers, the geological spread and the decentralized nature help in offering reliable services with coverage over a wide area. Fog computing is the physical location of the devices, which are much closer to the users than the cloud servers.

Last few years, cloud computing has been in the trend due to its computing, data storage, and network management functions. All these functions carry out in centralized data-centers. It has gained popularity among individuals and organizations being a cost-effective service and also it's increasing demand in diverse domains. This also led to a very effective global scaling of cloud computing. It can deliver the appropriate amount of resources at the exact geographic location. It also increased the productivity of an organization by reducing the number of chores required to be done by the IT teams. These became the results for cloud computing's increased performance, security, and reliability. The services of cloud computing are recognized as stacks of cloud computing, which are infrastructure as a service (IaaS), platform as a service (PaaS), and software as a service (SaaS). However, there are growing many challenges for cloud computing on the road ahead.

There has been a tremendous increase of the Internet connected devices over the past few years, which has led to high demand of IoT across the world. These centralized cloud data centers often fail to work with the billions of geographically distributed IoT devices. This framework of cloud computing is failing to provide real time services and often causing network congestion, high latency in quality of services. To support all these demands, Cisco introduced the concept of "Fog Computing." It is an extension of the Cloud based facilities and it stays much closer to the IoT nodes. This fog layer is simply a layer between the Cloud data centers and the End users. This layer has led to the decentralization of the data centers. This migration of cloud to the edge of network where the end device such as router itself becomes virtualized here and are called as "fog." Fog computing has started to become an urging need among individuals and organizations due to some its tremendous advantages. Some of them are:- support of real-time services, low latency, location awareness, support of mobility, geographic distribution, low-power consumption, less network congestion, processing high number of nodes, cost effective, reliable etc.

***Table 5.1:** Differences between Cloud and Fog Computing*

Feature	Cloud Computing	Fog Computing
Latency	Cloud computing has high latency compared to fog computing	Fog computing has low latency
Capacity	Cloud Computing does not provide any reduction in data while sending or transforming data	Fog Computing reduces the amount of data sent to cloud computing.
Responsivenes	Response time of the system is low.	Response time of the system is high.
Security	Cloud computing has less security compared to Fog Computing	Fog computing has high Security.
Speed	Access speed is high depending on the VM connectivity.	High even more compared to Cloud Computing.
Data Integration	Multiple data sources can be integrated.	Multiple Data sources and devices can be integrated.
Mobility	In cloud computing mobility is Limited.	Mobility is supported in fog computing.
Location Awareness	Partially Supported in Cloud computing.	Supported in fog computing.
Number of Server Nodes	Cloud computing has Few number of server nodes.	Fog computing has Large number of server nodes.
Geographical Distribution	It is centralized.	It is decentralized and distributed.
Location of service	Services provided within the internet.	Services provided at the edge of the local network.
Working environment	Specific data center building with air conditioning systems	Outdoor (streets,base stations, etc.) or indoor (houses, cafes, etc.)
Communication mode	IP network	Wireless communication: WLAN, WiFi, 3G, 4G, ZigBee, etc. or wired communication (part of the IP networks)
Dependence on the quality of core network	Requires strong network core.	Can also work in Weak network core.

Benefits of Fog Computing

- It is less expensive to operate with fog computing as data is hosted and analyzed on local devices rather than transferring it to any cloud device.
- It helps to facilitate and control business operation at par by deploying fog application as per the user's need.
- Fogging offer different choices to users for processing their data over any physical devices.

Associated Vehicles

- Self-driven cars are nowadays in a boom in the market. As a result, producing a remarkable volume of data.
- The data needs to be look over quickly based on the information provided like traffic, driving conditions, etc. All this is done quickly with the help of fog computing.

Smart Grids and Smart Cities

- To increase the potentiality of management of systems energy networks need to use real- time data.
- It is also important to execute the remote data near the place where it is produced.
- Therefore, these issues can be addressed using fog computing.

Real-time Analytics

- Data can be transferred from place to place from where it is created using fog computing.
- Fog computing is using real-time analytics that passes data from the production organizations to the financial institutions.

5.2 Cloud to Fog Architecture

A typical fog computing architecture is given below. There are several layers mentioned in the same Figure and it is composed of the networking devices such as routers, set-top boxes, proxy servers, base stations, etc. All these devices store frequently used information to provide the services to edge user.

- Level 1 demonstrates the End Devices/ End Users, where all the IoT enabled devices are known as Terminal Nodes are taking services from the cloud/fog server.
- Level 2 is the actual fog computing layer. This layer consists of the fog nodes in the form of routers, set-top boxes, proxy servers, base stations, etc. These nodes have storage facilities and as well as computation capability.
- Level 3 is the cloud computing layer. All the cloud data centers and cloud servers reside in this layer and they have storage and computing facilities.

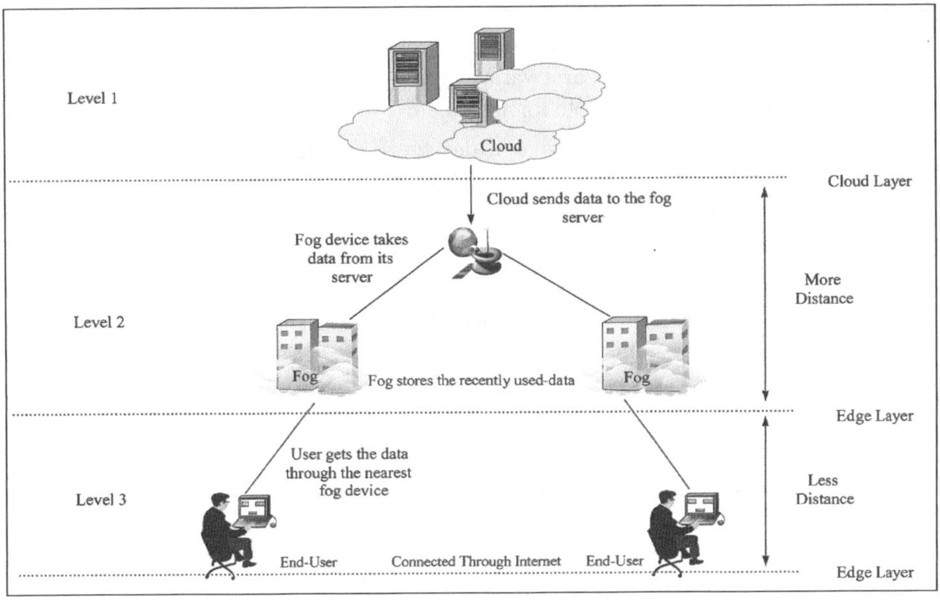

Fig. 5.1: Fog Computing

5.2.1 User roles

User lies at the lowest level/tier of a typical fog computing environment. User will have to access the data from the fog nodes (networking devices) which are decentralized and provides localized information.

But, if the required data is not available in fog devices, then the user will directly access cloud storage of the cloud server. Note that, the data may or may not sensitive. But, some cryptographic mechanism is required to protect the public/private data.

5.2.2 Fog devices role

Fog is the intermediate level/tier between the user and Cloud layer. It is the most important layer for computing purposes. It usually consists of the fog nodes in the form of routers, set-top boxes, proxy servers, base stations, etc.

Here, the fog nodes receive the data from the centralized data centers of the cloud if it is not meet the user requirement. After that, it transmits the data received to the end users with the help of the fog nodes and it makes the data decentralized and localized. The users can easily retrieve the data from the fog nodes through Internet Communication

5.2.3 Cloud server roles

Cloud is the topmost level/tier of a typical fog computing environment. This level consists of centralized data centers, which has the capacity to store all the data of the fog nodes/servers. It has usually the capacity to store a huge amount of data. It causes huge network congestion and also it causes high latency in quality of services.

5.2.4 Fog Deployment Models

We may distinguish fog models based on the ownership of the fog infrastructure and underlying properties. We have four different types of fog models:

- **Private fog:** A private fog is developed, purchased, maintained and controlled by an entity, a third entity or a variation thereof. It can be installed on or off-site. Private fog services are sold for absolute use by a single company.
- **Public fog:** A public fog is owned, developed, and managed by, or a combination of, a corporation, academic institution or government organization. It is deployed on the premises of the fog suppliers. Public fog services are provided for open access by the common or general public.
- **Community fog:** Community fog is developed, maintained and controlled by different community organizations, which may include a third party too, or a consolidation of them.

  It can be installed on or off-premises and services are provided for exclusive use, typically by customers in a particular group of organizations with common interests.
- **Hybrid fog:** Hybrid fog is a type of cloud computing that incorporates the use of public/private/community fog with public/private cloud computing (i.e., hybrid cloud).

  It may be helpful due to the disadvantages of the physical resources in the fog. As a result, the platform is applied to the hybrid cloud to scale performance.

5.3 Disadvantages of Fog Computing

- **Complexity:** Different modules from both the edge and the central network can make use of a possible Fog computing framework. Usually, these modules are Equipped with different types of processors but not us ed for general purpose computation.

  Owing to its ambiguity, it can be difficult to grasp the principle of Fog computing. There are several computers placed at various locations that store and evaluate their own data collection. This could bring more complexity to the network. In addition, more advanced fog nodes exist in the fog infrastructure.
- **Security:** Authentic entry to services and privacy in Fog computing are difficult to ensure. There are various devices and different fog nodes in the fog computing environment. These fog nodes are likely to be in a less secure environment. Hackers can conveniently use bogus IP addresses to obtain access to the corresponding fog node.
- **Power Consumption:** There are many fog nodes available in the fog environment that is directly proportional to their energy consumption. That implies that these fog nodes need a high volume of energy to work. If the fog infrastructure requires more fog nodes, there is even more power usage.
- **Authentication:** The service delivered by fog computing is on a wide scale. Fog networking is made up of end-users, Internet service providers, and cloud providers. This will also pose concerns about trust and authentication in the fog.

5.4 Applications of Fog Computing

It is useful in various IoT applications. A large range of sensors can be mounted in the sea, airline fleets or a car, so it's difficult to dispatch and reserve all data produced instantaneous in the cloud. A few interim computing, analysis and processing will be provided by Fog Computing appliances.

Connected Vehicle: There are several useful qualities that rely on fog and Internet access which is applied to vehicles, like automatic transmission and "hands-free" operation or vehicle that is capable of parking itself, which means, no requirement for a human being to park a vehicle. As part of the Intelligent Transport System, vehicle communication has been designed to achieve protection and efficiency through intelligent transportation by incorporating a variety of information. Connections in an intelligent transport system are accomplished by different communications variations which is vehicle- to-vehicle (V2V) and many a times vehicle-toinfrastructure (V2I). Fog computing is the highly capable approach for all Internet connections. Vehicles, as they have a high degree of real-time interaction., it will encourage vehicles, traffic lights and access points to exchange communication with each other in order to provide a reliable service to users.

- **Smart Traffic Lights:** Fog computing enables road signals to be opened based on the sensing of blinking lights. It detects the appearance of bikes and pedestrians and monitors the speed and distance between vehicles in the vicinity. Sensor lighting is turned on as it detects motions and vice versa Fog computing enables traffic signals to clear roads based on the sensing of blinking lights.
- **Augmented Reality:** Augmented - reality technologies are highly delay sensitive; a minor delay will result in significant errors in user interface. Therefore, Fog

computing-based technologies will have tremendous potential in this area. Zao et al. proposed an improved interaction game for brain computers using Fog and cloud infrastructure.

- **Smart HealthCare:** Because of pollution our surroundings have various kinds of bacteria and viruses which causes various diseases. Smart healthcare includes smart IoT, which is capable of tracking the activities of patients and keeps track of various parameters of their body and uploads the data on the fog nodes, and these are being noticed by the medical staffs and then appropriate measures are suggested by the doctors to the patients.
- **Waste management:** The earth is getting polluted every day. To save the earth, we need to focus on natural resources. Rising waste and water loss from the ground needs significant consideration. Smart garbage management may be considered as one of the solutions for the improvement of the environment.

5.5 Fog Computing Architecture

Fog computing decentralize the computing infrastructure without depending on centralize computing such as cloud computing. Fog computing is a paradigm proposed to integrate IoT and cloud concept to support user mobility, low latency and location awareness. Fog computing (also known as edge computing) deploys datacenters in the network edges, it offers location awareness, low latency, and improves qualityof-services (QoS) for near real-time applications.

Typical examples include transportation, industrial automation, agriculture and other smart cities applications. Fog infrastructure supports heterogeneous devices, such as end device, edge devices, access points, and switches. Fog servers are considered as micro datacenter by inheriting cloud services to network edges. The datacenters positioned for near real-time applications, big data analytics, distributed data collection, and offers advantages in various applications in smart cities.

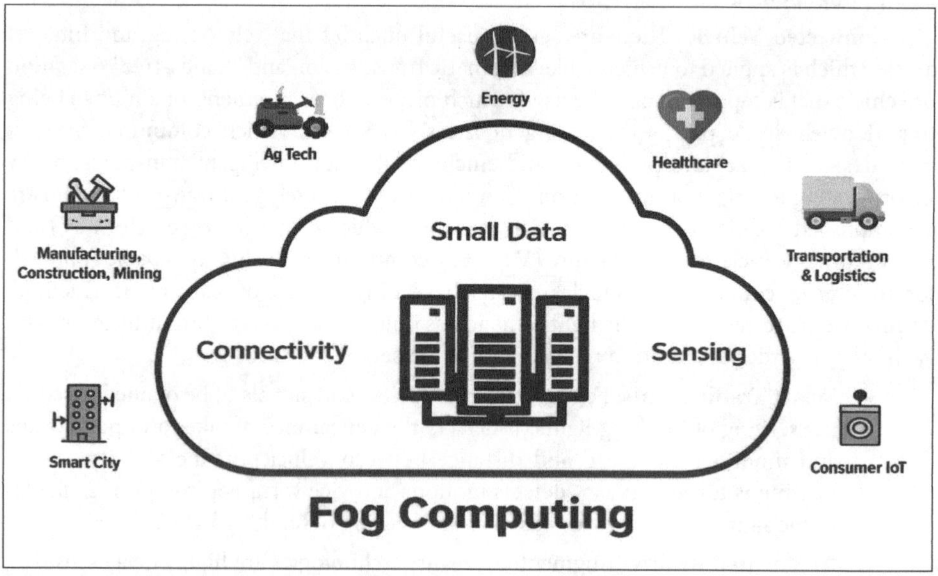

Fig. 5.2: Fog Computing

5.5.1 Three Layer Architecture of Fog Computing

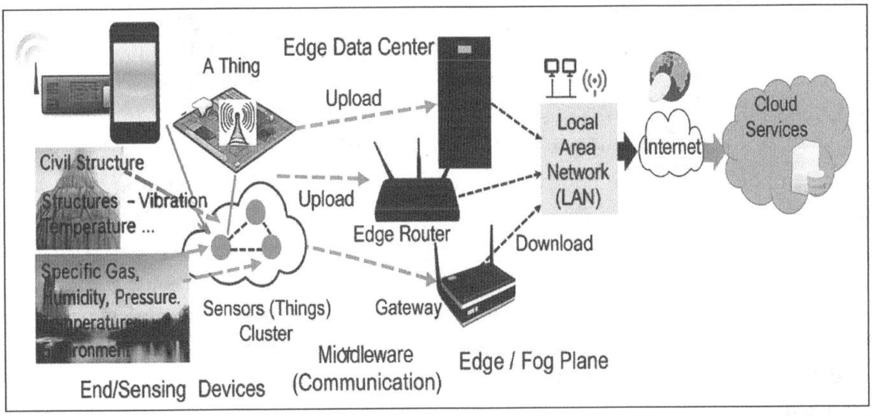

Fig. 5.3: Fog Computing Architecture is implemented in two predominant Models

5.5.2 Hierarchical Architecture Model

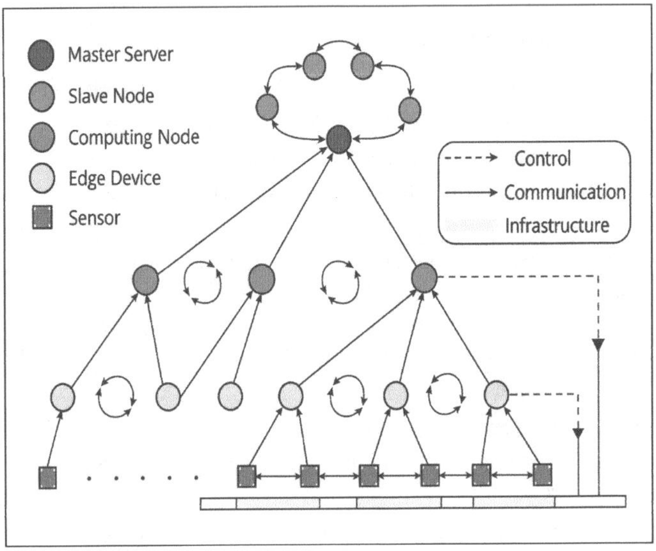

Fig. 5.4: Hierarchical Architectural model

This model of cloud computing uses the fundamental three-layer structure in a hierarchical form of architecture. The three layers comprise of:

1. Terminal Layer

The terminal layer is the fundamental layer in the fog design, which comprises devices such as cell phones, cameras, smart cars, readers, smart cards, etc.The sensors in this layer can detect and collect data that is present in the network. Devices are distributed widely away from each other over a range of locations.The layer deals more with sensing and collecting data. In this segment, devices from various platforms and various architectures are primarily found.Applications have the potential to run in a heterogeneous environment, with other devices utilizing distinct technologies and different communication modes.

2. Fog Layer

The Fog layer contains equipment called Fog nodes, such as routers, gateways, entry points, base stations, individual fog servers, etc.The fog nodes are placed at the edge of a network. An edge may be a hop away from the end of the unit. These nodes are located between Cloud Data Centers and End Devices.Fog nodes can be static, such as those in a bus terminal or coffee shop, or they can be shifted, such as those inside a moving car.

These nodes supply the end devices with facilities. It can also temporarily compute, transmit and store the data.

3. Cloud Layer

This layer consists of computers that can provide high performance with massive storage and machines (servers).The cloud layer conducts the study of computations and permanently saves data for backup and remains persistent user controlIt has a high capacity for storage and efficient computation.

A cloud layer is created by enormous data centers with high processing ability. These data centers provide customers with all the fundamental features of cloud computing. The data centers are both flexible and have on-demand computing services.

5.5.3 Layered Architecture Model

This model of the architecture of Fog computing consists of six concise layers:

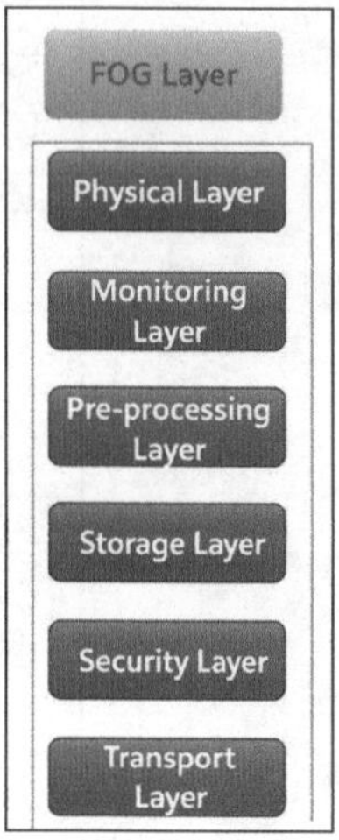

***Fig. 5.5:** Layered Architecture Model*

- **Physical and Virtualisation layer**: The first stage consists of physical and virtual nodes as well as sensors. These sensors are distributed geographically to sense the environment and retrieve data.
- **Monitoring Layer:** In this layer, the then received nodes and sensors will be monitored thoroughly. At what time and where the fog node performed the tasks will be observed. Another key feature that will be monitored is the energy consumption of the nodes.
- **Pre-processing Layer**: This layer collects, analyzes, and trims data to get meaningful insights. After which the data is stored securely.
- **Temporary storage Layer:** This is where the pre-processed data will be stored. Here performance-elevating activities such as data distribution, replication, deduplication, and virtualization of storage spaces are performed.
- **Security Layer:** In this segment, the data received is sent for processing, encryption, and decryption. It also ensures privacy and integrity measures are followed religiously.
- **Transport layer:** When the final layer receives the information its main objective is to upload pre-processed and secure data to the cloud. The final stage of the layered Fog Computing Architecture sends the data to the cloud which is then stored and used to create services for users.

Fog Computing has gradually yet efficiently taken over data adaptations of devices. Here are **some of the advantages** of this form of Computing:

- **Enhanced user experience:** As data is analyzed locally and then transmitted to the cloud there are fewer technical errors and provides instant responses. Which will in turn increase the satisfaction amongst users.
- **No bandwidth issues:** Instead of providing large sums of unfiltered data, this computing architectural method transmits only accurate and necessary data to the cloud source.
- **Improved response time:** Real-time applications will benefit largely from live and instant responses. This is because the Fog Nodes are placed remotely around the data source and also because there are minimal shutdowns and system failures in the network.
- **Security and Data Privacy:** Fog Computing handles the data processed in the network with the ultimate security features and also ensures all sensitive data is withheld and processed locally. This ensures that no data is tampered with or misused. This is done by protecting the Fog Nodes through policies and controls established amongst the network.

5.6 Edge Computing

Edge computing is a distributed, open IT architecture that features decentralized processing power, enabling mobile computing and Internet of Things (IoT) technologies. In edge computing, data is processed by the device itself or by a local computer or server, rather than being transmitted to a data center.

This proximity to data at its source can deliver strong business benefits, including faster insights, improved response times and better bandwidth availability.Edge can relate to data processing as well as local processing of the real time data. The various edge components that can be counted upon are:

1. Data processing, Rule Engine, Local Database. Amazon (NASDAQ:AMZN),
2. Microsoft (NASDAQ:MSFT), and
3. **Alphabet (NASDAQ:GOOGL)(NASDAQ:GOOG):** All three of these tech giants' cloud offerings -- Amazon Web Services, Microsoft Azure, and Google Cloud -- support edge computing in both hardware and software

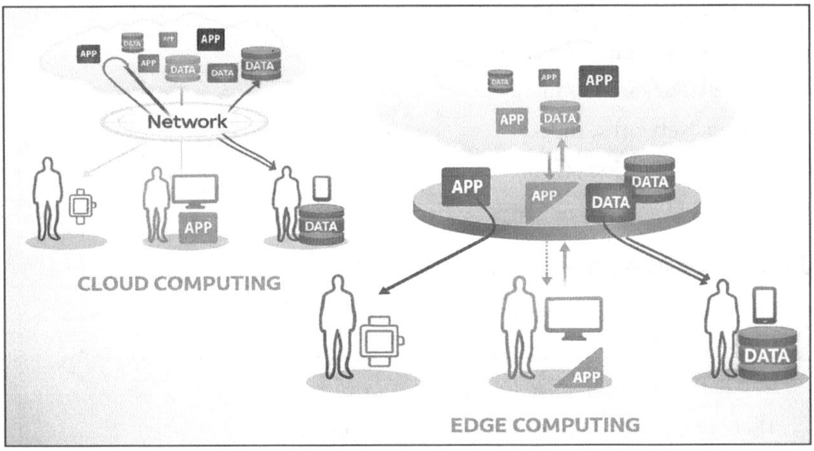

Fig. 5.6: Edge Computing

This technology increases the efficient usage of bandwidth by analysing the data at edges itself unlike the cloud which requires transfer of data from the IOT requiring large bandwidth, making it useful to be used in remote location with minimum cost.It allows smart applications and devices to respond to data almost at the same time which is important in terms of business ad self driving cars.It has the ability to process data without even putting on a public cloud, this ensures full security. Data might get corrupt while on an extended network thus affecting the data reliability for the industries to use.Edge computation of data provides a limitation to the use of cloud.

Edge is more specific towards computational processes for the edge devices. So, fog includes edge computing, but would also include the network for the processed data to its final destination.

Key Benefits Of Edge Computing

- Faster response time.
- Security and Compliance.
- Cost-effective Solution.
- Reliable Operation With Intermittent Connectivity.

Edge Cloud Computing Services

- IOT (Internet Of Things)
- Gaming
- Health Care
- Smart City
- Intelligent Transportation
- Enterprise Security

10 Companies in Edge Computing Market

- Microsoft Corporation....
- IBM Corporation....
- Huawei Technologies Co., Ltd....
- Dell Technologies, Inc....
- Hewlett-Packard Company....
- Juniper Networks, Inc....
- Cisco Systems, Inc....
- Google LLC.

Disadvantages of a Peer to Peer Network

- The files or resources are not centrally organized with a P2P network....
- Virus introduction risks rise with a peer to peer network....
- P2P networks often have very little security....
- There is no way to back up files or folders centrally.

Pros of P2P	Cons of P2P
Easy to apply and shop for	Can be risky if not done cautiously
Low interest rates	May not cover your full investment price

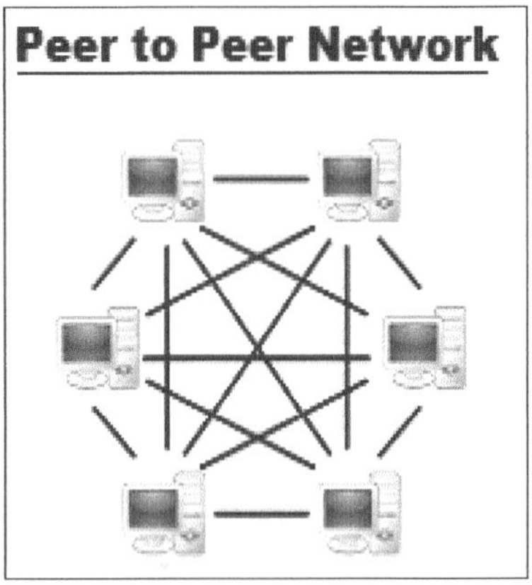

Fig. 5.7: *Peer to Peer network*

Torrent: Torrent is a big example of a P2P network. In torrent, all the computers are connected to each other on the internet. One computer can upload any file in the network and other computers start downloading the files.

Because users can control access to files and resources on their computers, network administration isn't controlled by one person. As such, peer-to-peer networks are generally used in small deployments and in situations where security isn't a major concern, as in the case of home networks or small businesses.

As a centralized, proprietary, walled garden service, Facebook is a single point for attacks, control, and surveillance, never mind controversial policies or privacy concerns. Facebook may enable a more bottom-up and peer-to-peer network compared to many things

List of Peer-to-Peer (P2P) File Sharing Applications

- Xunlei.
- Bittorrent, uTorrent, BitComet, Vuze and Transmission.
- Azureus.
- Emule and eDonkey.
- Gnutella, LimeWire and Cabos.
- WinMX.
- Share.
- Winny.

Characteristics of Peer to Peer Networks

A peer-to-peer (p2p) network provides a scalable and fault-tolerant mechanism to locate nodes anywhere on a network without maintaining large amount of routing state. This allows for a variety of applications beyond simple file sharing, including in multicast systems, anonymous communications systems, and web caches.

Types of P2P networks

- Pure P2P Network: Using this kind of P2P network, not a dedicated server, is considered, where each peer in the network plays an equal role....
- Unstructured P2P Networks:...
- Structured P2P Network:...
- Hybrid P2P Network:

Based on network design, a computer network can be divided into the following two types:

1. Peer-to-Peer Network
2. Server-Based Network

A Server-Based network can also be termed as a Client-Server network. A server is a node that acts as a service provider for clients. They wait for client requests and then respond to them. The server is located elsewhere on the network, usually on a more powerful machine. Here, the server is the central location where users share and access network resources. It controls the level of access that users have to share resources. In other words, a server provides functionality and serve other programs called clients.

The Peer-to-Peer network is also called P2P or computer-to-computer network. 'Peers' are the nodes or computer system which are connected to each other. In this kind of network, each node is connected to each other node in the network.

The nodes can share printers or CDROM drives, and allow other devices to read or write to its hard disk, allowing sharing of files, access to its internet connection, and other resources. Files or resources can be shared directly between the system on the network, without the need of any central server. Such kind of network, where we allow nodes to become a server and share things in this manner, can be referred to as a peer-to-peer network.

In a peer-to-peer network, each node can work as either a server as well as a client. This network does not distinguish between the client or server. Each of the nodes can act as both client/server depending on whether the node is requesting or providing the service. All the nodes are functionally equal and can send or receive data directly with one another.

Peer-to-Peer networks can be deployed very easily with most modern Operating Systems such as Windows and Mac O.S., etc. Computers in the peer-to-peer network run the same network protocols and software. Once connected to the network, P2P software allows users to search for files and other resources on some other node. The pattern of communication between peers depends entirely on the application requirement. Each object is replicated in several computers to further distribute the load and to provide flexibility in the event of disconnection of the individual computer.

Advantages of Using a Peer-to-Peer Network

1. Easy to implement and manage.
2. Nodes or workstations are independent of one another. Also, no access permissions are needed.
3. The network is reliable in nature. If a peer fails, it will not affect the working of others.
4. There is no need for any professional software in such kind of networks.
5. The cost of implementation of such networks is very less.

Disadvantages of Using a Peer-to-Peer Network

1. Storage is decentralized, and also not so efficiently managed.
2. No data backup options are available in peer-to-peer networks.
3. These kinds of networks are not so secure.

Security and Privacy in Fog

One of the main concerns regarding the security and privacy in cloud computing is the protection of data.... If the security and privacy in cloud computing is neglected, then the private information of each user is at risk, allowing easy cyber breaches to hack into the system and exploit any users' private storage data.

How Does Fog Computing Reduces Security Risks?

There being a higher probability for security issues when large amounts of data are transferred through networks, fog computing reduces the amount of data being transferred back and forth to the cloud, hence, reducing latency as a result of local computation while minimizing security risks.

How Fog Provide Better Privacy to Industries and Companies?

Fog nodes allow the expansion of power for cloud computing, and benefit companies in the following way: Greater business agility.... Deeper insights and privacy control: Data is analysed locally instead of sending it to the cloud for analysis; Fog allows to control devices that collect, analyse and store data.

5.7 Security Concerns

The fog server in general provides resources to the end-user. So, it is mandatory that the fog server should first check the authenticity of the end user and then provides resources securely. In this mechanism, unauthorized access is possible, that means no malicious user could not access the fog services. Password based authentication technique is one of the existing mechanisms that protects unauthorized access and provides data communication securely after exchanging key between the entities. Therefore security protocol for authentication that must provide mutual authentication security aspects. In order to design such types of authentication protocol, security protection on several security attacks are challenging issues and must provide in the protocol.

These security attacks are password guessing issue attack, man-in-the-middle attack, insider issue attack, session key recovery attack, impersonation attack, gateway compromise attack, replay attack and most important security aspects are mutual authentication, perfect forward secrecy.

5.7.1 Authentication Concern

Authentication techniques are one of the main issues of security services and it is indeed required in cloud-fog computing archi- tecture. The end-user(s) or device(s) must be authenticated to the receiver-end (such as server) before accessing any resources. n this model, authen- tication plays an important role, because fog devices can provide services after only end-user authentication and similarly, the cloud server must also authenticate end- user as well as fog devices before providing permission for accessing resources.

These techniques are called basically one-way authentication. But, due to large volume of networks and cloud masquerade attack, mutual authentication is also equally important. Resembling man-in-the-middle attack, it is also extremely important security issues in mutual authentication protocol, where the attacker attempts to impersonate as either end user or fog serve. If this attack executes by the attacker in some way, the valid entity (end user, fog server) will suffer from getting the original message. So, protecting such type of attack is highly desirable.

Another important thing in cloud-fog computing model is to establish secure communication between end-user, fog devices and cloud server. In this context, an adversary may launch several security threats. Hence, it is also very imperative and challenging research issues to design an robust authentication protocol for cloud-fog computing model.

Maintaining high-entropy passwords set for set of accounts is really hard job for the users and hence they either use a common password or low-entropy password. Low-entropy password is basically a dictionary word which is easily guessable by using cryptographic techniques. So, password protection is an important issue in password based authentication system.

If the password is disclosed or can calculate by the attacker, it is very easy to break the security system. Hence, password protection is important issue in this security framework.

According to the literature report, most of the security system breaks due to insider issue where the system administrator discloses vital security factors of the client such as password to the third parties. So, the mutual authentication protocol should be designed in such a way that the insider person could not able to retrieve client's confidential information.

The cloud-fog computing model is basically three-layer architecture. Hence, one of the security concerns is man-in-the-middle attack. It is a common attack in many applications such as smart grid, wireless sensor network, cloud computing, fog computing, medical environment, etc., where the attacker traps the messages from the source end and makes modification and forwards another message to the receiver end to break the security system.

The malicious user can trap the message from the user end and can forward another valid/invalid message to the fog server. This attack can also be launch between the fog and cloud servers. Therefore, protecting this attack is an important security issues.

In replay the attacker plainly retrieves message from the sender and forwards identical message to receiver to launch this attack. At a standstill, there is no efficient cryptographic mechanism which can protect reply attack. One of the existing way out to protect it is timestamp technique.

But, it is not suitable for distributed environment due to time synchronization issue. So, security protection is essential to protect reply attack. Perfect forward secrecy property is highly important in any cryptographic protocols.

Because, if the private key of the entities is disclosed in some ways to the attacker, the security of the previously established encrypted key should not disclosed..

5.7.2 Data integrity

The concept of data integrity confirms that the message receives by the receiver-end exactly same of which the sender sent. It is also one of the important properties which is required in cloud-fog computing model. The end-user is generally accessed data from either fog or cloud server. While the fog or cloud server sends the required data, it is necessary to provide the data integrity. In the same way, if the end-user wants to send data to either fog device or cloud server, the integrity should be preserved. One of the existing techniques of cryptography called hash function (Example: SHA-1, SHA-2, MD5, etc.) is used to provide integrity property. Several researchers have been worked on it and try to achieve strong integrity property. To best of our knowledge, still strong integrity as well as efficient complexity are open research challenges for the cloud-fog computing model.

5.7.3 Secure data storage

Data storage either in server or cloud in plaintext form is a very simple issues, but to store data securely, it is very open challenging research and still researchers are working on it. In our cloud-fog computing model, the valuable data is stored in fog devices (frequently used data) and also in cloud server. Both fog and cloud server maintain database for storing data. In the context of fog computing, the data are stored in fog-database for future use. But, the challenge is that how the fog devices will provide security on stored data. It is known to all that adversary has the high capabilities or they used high-standard techniques to break the security system.

We are assuming that the data is stored as plainest in fog device. If it is happening then the adversary can physically compromise fog device to get the stored valuable data. On the other hand, several researchers have been proposed to store the data in encrypted mode so that they cannot decrypt the data upon getting the stored encrypted data. In this regard, the fog devices have to maintain keys for encrypting and decryption.

Similar to fog devices, the same types of issues are there in cloud computing. To the best of our knowledge, it is still a open challenge in research community to store data securely with efficient performance of the algorithm.

5.8 Security and Privacy Issues and Solutions of Fog Computing

What are the security and privacy issues that face Fog computing has created a new dilemma of security and privacy-related issues due to its notable characteristics of distribution, heterogeneity, mobility, and limited resources. It would be difficult for the Fog to execute a full suite of security solutions that can detect and prevents attacks due to its relatively low computing power. Also, due to its location (ie, close to IoT devices which means protection and surveillance are relatively weak), the Fog will be easier and more accessible than the Cloud, which increases the probability of attacks.

In addition, Fog will be an attractive target to many attacks, due to its ability to obtain sensitive data from both IoT devices and the Cloud, and due to the amount of throughput data.

Therefore, Fog nodes may encounter several malicious attacks (eg, man-in-the-middle, authentication, distributed denial of services DDOS attacks, access control, and fault tolerance) and new security and privacy challenges. Moreover, while the Cloud has standard security and privacy measures and certifications, the Fog does not have such standards. Hence, the available security and privacy solutions that work for the Cloud may not work efficiently for the Fog.

5.8.1 Security and Privacy Threats

Since the Fog is an extension to Cloud computing, it inherits many threats from the Cloud. Moreover, Fog nodes are "honest but curious" in general.This is because these nodes are deployed by Fog vendors who are honest in providing certain services to end-users. However, they may snoop on the content and personal data of the end-users. The providers of Fog may ask the end-users for personal information in order to maintain or fix some issues, which might lead to leakage in the user's privacy. In addition, Fog nodes are an attractive target for many types of attacks. Table 1 summarizes the different attacks that may occur on Fog nodes.

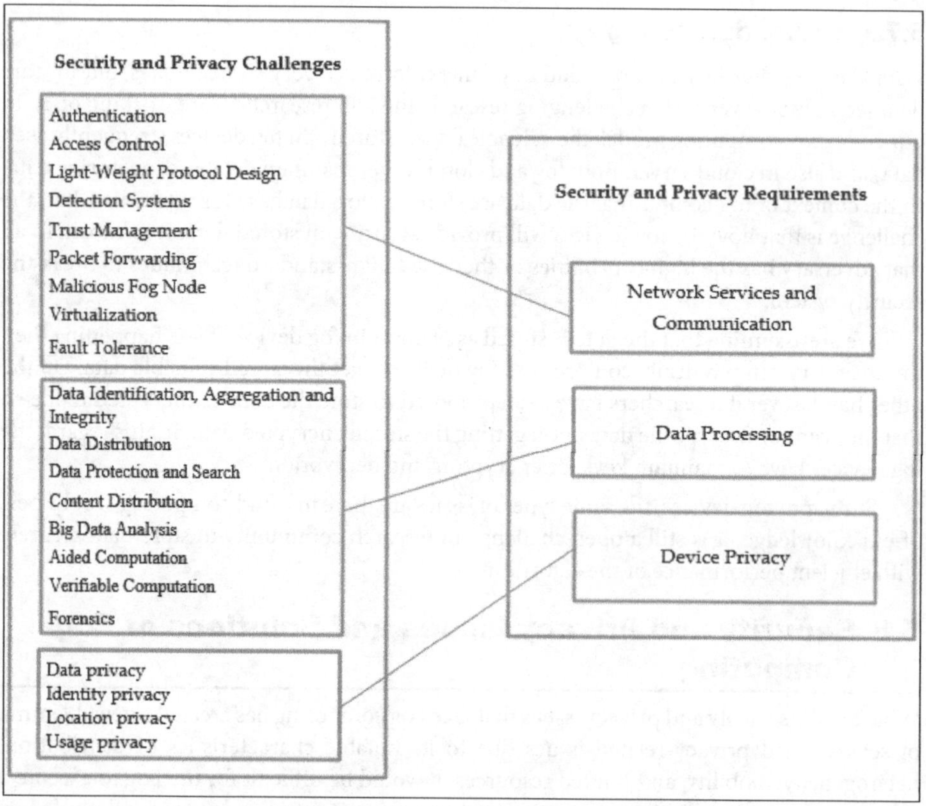

Fig. 5.8: Security and Privacy Requirements

The three essential requirements of security and privacy are confidentiality of data transmission and storage, the integrity and availability of data. Confidentiality ensures that only the data owner (ie, IoT device user) can access the data. This prevents unauthorized access while data are transmitted or received among the device layer, Fog layer, core network, and when data are stored or processed in Fog or Cloud data centers.

Confidentiality can be attained by data encryption. Integrity ensures that the data delivered is correct and consistent without distortion or undetected modification. It also prevents the data stored from modification or distortion. Data integrity checking mechanisms can be used to ensure the consistency between sent data and received data. Availability ensures that the data are available and accessible by authorized parties (e.g., anywhere and anytime) as per users' requirements.

To achieve these requirements, different tools, techniques, procedures, and strategies (eg, authentication, encryption) should be applied in different layers during data transmission and storing.

EXERCISE

A. Objective Questions

1. What is Fog Computing?
   (a) A type of cloud computing focused on data storage
   (b) A distributed computing model that extends cloud computing closer to the edge devices
   (c) A networking model used in traditional data centers
   (d) A method of internet security
2. What is the main advantage of Fog Computing over traditional cloud computing?
   (a) Increased centralized data storage
   (b) Reduced latency and faster processing near the data source
   (c) Higher dependence on centralized servers
   (d) Lower data privacy
3. In Fog Computing Architecture, which of the following is responsible for local data processing?
   (a) Cloud servers (b) Fog nodes/devices
   (c) Data centers (d) End-user devices
4. What is the primary role of Fog Devices?
   (a) Performing complex analytics
   (b) Storing data permanently
   (c) Processing data closer to the source before sending it to the cloud
   (d) Replacing cloud computing completely
5. Which of the following is a major disadvantage of Fog Computing?
   (a) High latency
   (b) Increased security risks due to distributed nature
   (c) Heavy reliance on centralized servers
   (d) Reduced scalability
6. Edge Computing is different from Fog Computing because:
   (a) It stores data in a centralized cloud
   (b) It focuses solely on security measures
   (c) It processes data directly at the end-user device rather than intermediate fog nodes
   (d) It does not support IoT applications
7. Which security concern in Fog Computing involves verifying user identity?
   (a) Authentication concerns
   (b) Secure data storage
   (c) Data integrity
   (d) Deployment models

8. The main challenge of secure data storage in Fog Computing is:
   (a) Limited access to cloud-based storage
   (b) Unauthorized access and data breaches
   (c) Over-reliance on internet connectivity
   (d) Excessive data redundancy
9. Which of the following is not a common security threat in Fog Computing?
   (a) Man-in-the-middle attacks (b) Data encryption
   (c) Denial-of-Service (DoS) attacks (d) Unauthorized access
10. Which security approach is used to protect data integrity in Fog Computing?
   (a) Public Wi-Fi networks (b) Hashing algorithms and blockchain
   (c) Open-access data transfers (d) Weak authentication methods

B. Subjective Questions

1. Define Fog Computing and explain its role in modern computing infrastructure.
2. Compare Fog Computing and Cloud Computing in terms of latency, security, and processing efficiency.
3. Describe the Cloud to Fog Architecture and explain how data is transferred between layers.
4. What are the key components of Fog Computing Architecture?
5. Explain the role of user devices, fog nodes, and cloud servers in a Fog Computing system.
6. List and explain the major applications of Fog Computing in real-world industries.
7. What are the key disadvantages of Fog Computing? How can they be mitigated?
8. How does Fog Computing enhance IoT applications compared to traditional cloud computing?
9. Explain the relationship between Edge Computing and Fog Computing.
10. Explain the concept of authentication concerns in a Fog Computing environment.